Business Result

SECOND EDITION

Upper-intermediate *Teacher's Book*

Rachel Appleby &
John Hughes

OXFORD
UNIVERSITY PRESS

Great Clarendon Street, Oxford, OX2 6DP, United Kingdom

Oxford University Press is a department of the University of Oxford.
It furthers the University's objective of excellence in research, scholarship,
and education by publishing worldwide. Oxford is a registered trade
mark of Oxford University Press in the UK and in certain other countries

© Oxford University Press 2018

The moral rights of the author have been asserted

First published in 2018

2022 2021 2020

10 9 8 7 6 5 4 3

ISBN: 978 0 19 473902 3   Book
ISBN: 978 0 19 473901 6   Pack

Printed in China

This book is printed on paper from certified and well-managed sources

ACKNOWLEDGEMENTS

Cover image: Getty Images/Steve Debenport

Back cover photograph: Oxford University Press building/David Fisher

*The authors and publisher would like to thank Saïd Business School for their assistance
in producing the Viewpoint video interviews on the Teacher's Book DVD. In particular,
we would like to thank the following people for their time, assistance and expertise*:
Nazia Ali, Ahmed Abu Bakr, Lydia Darley, Louise Fitzgerald, Kathy Harvey,
Thomas Hellmann, Sophie Kin Seong, Georgia Lewis, Tim Morris, Ana María
Ñungo, Thomas Pilsworth, Andy Poole, Josie Powell, Nancy Puccinelli, Hiram
Samel, Andrew Stephen, Breanne Svehla, Jonathan Trevor, Peter Tufano, John
Walugembe.

Contents

Introduction

The course

Who is *Business Result Second Edition* for?

Business Result Second Edition is a comprehensive multi-level course in business English suitable for a wide range of learners. The main emphasis is on *enabling* your students, helping them to communicate more effectively in their working lives.

In-work students

Unlike many business English courses, *Business Result Second Edition* addresses the language and communication needs of employees at all levels of an organization, who need to use English at work. It recognizes that the business world is truly international and that many people working in a modern, global environment spend much of their time doing everyday tasks in English – communicating with colleagues and work contacts by phone, via email and in a range of face-to-face situations, such as formal and informal meetings/discussions, and various planned and unplanned social encounters. The course contains topics and activities that allow the students to participate in a way that is relevant to them, whatever their level in their company or organization.

Pre-work learners

Business Result Second Edition can also be used with pre-work learners at college level. The course covers a variety of engaging topics over the 15 units, so students without much work experience will receive a wide-ranging overview of the business world, as well as acquiring the key communication skills they will need in their future working lives. Each unit in this *Teacher's Book* contains suggestions for adapting the material to the needs of these students.

One-to-one teaching

Many of the activities in the book are designed for use with groups of students, but they can also be easily adapted to suit a one-to-one teaching situation. Teaching notes in the *Teacher's Book* units offer suggestions and help with this.

What approach does *Business Result Second Edition* take?

Business Result Second Edition helps students communicate in English in real-life work situations. The priority at all times is on enabling them to do so more effectively and with confidence. The target language in each unit has been carefully selected to ensure that students will be equipped with genuinely useful, transferable language that they can take out of the classroom and use immediately in the workplace.

The course recognizes that, with so many businesses now being staffed by people of different nationalities, there is an increasing trend towards using English as the language of internal communication in many organizations. As well as learning appropriate language for communicating externally – with clients or suppliers, for example – students are also given the opportunity to practise in situations that take place within an organization, such as giving a report, making arrangements and taking part in meetings.

The main emphasis of the course is on the students speaking and trying out the target language in meaningful and authentic ways; it is expected that a large proportion of the lesson time will be spent on activating students' interest and encouraging them to talk. The material intentionally takes a communicative, heads-up approach, maximizing the amount of classroom time available to focus on and practise the target language. However, you will also find that there is plenty of support in terms of reference notes, written practice and review material.

The syllabus is essentially communication-driven. The topics in each of the 15 units have been chosen because of their relevance to modern business and the world of work. Vocabulary is presented in realistic contexts with reference to real companies or organizations. Grammar is also a key element of each unit. It is presented in an authentic context and ensures that students pay attention to accuracy, as well as becoming more proficient at expressing themselves clearly and precisely. The *Business communication* sections ensure that students are provided with a range of key expressions they can use immediately, both in the classroom and in their day-to-day work.

STUDENT'S BOOK

The *Student's Book* pack

The *Student's Book* pack offers a blend of classroom teaching and self-study, with an emphasis on flexibility and time-efficiency. Each of the 15 *Student's Book* units provides around four hours of classroom material with the potential for two to three hours of additional study using other materials in the pack.

The materials that support the *Student's Book* units are:
- *Viewpoint* video lessons
- Practice files
- Progress tests
- Photocopiable worksheets
- *Online practice*

More information on all of these materials and how to use them can be found in these Introduction pages.

Key features of a unit

Starting point

Each unit opens with some lead-in questions to raise awareness of, and interest in, the unit theme. Use these questions to help you establish what students already know about the topic and how it relates to their own working lives. These questions can usually be discussed as a class or in small groups.

Working with words

This first main section introduces key vocabulary in a variety of ways, including authentic reading texts, listening texts and visuals. Students are encouraged to look at how different forms of words (e.g. verbs, adjectives and nouns) can be built from the same root, or look at common combinations (e.g. verb + noun, adjective + noun) that will help them to expand their personal lexicon more rapidly. This section also offers opportunities to work on your students' reading and listening skills.

Business communication

This section focuses on one of five broad communication themes – meetings, presenting, exchanging information, phone calls and socializing. These are treated differently throughout the book so that, for example, students are able to practise exchanging information on the phone as well as face-to-face, or compare the different language needed for giving formal and informal presentations. Typically, the section begins with students listening to an example situation (a meeting, a presentation, a social encounter, a series of phone calls). They focus on *Key expressions* used by the speakers which are listed on the page. They are then given the opportunity to practise these in various controlled and more open work-related tasks.

Practically speaking

This section looks at various practical aspects of everyday communication and social interaction from a 'how to' perspective.

Language at work

The grammar is looked at from a communicative point of view; this will meet your students' expectations with regard to learning form and meaning, but also reminds them how the grammar they need to learn commonly occurs in business and work situations. The *Language point* highlights the target grammar structures, which are then practised in authentic work contexts.

Tips

Throughout each unit, there are short, practical tips with useful language points arising from a particular section or exercise.

Talking point

The *Talking point* at the end of the unit provides the opportunity for students to discuss a range of business concepts, approaches and ideas and how they might apply these in their own work. All of the topics relate to the unit theme and provide another opportunity for students to use the language from the unit. The *Talking point* generally follows a three-part structure: Input (via a short text, listening or infographic), Discussion, Task. In *Unit 10* the *Talking point* is presented as a game. This is designed to be fun and is aimed at recycling the language from the unit.

Viewpoint

After every three units there is a two-page *Viewpoint* video lesson. The topic of the *Viewpoint* lesson relates to a theme from the preceding units and includes authentic interviews with leading business experts from Saïd Business School in the University of Oxford. Each lesson opens with a focus on the topic supported by discussion questions. Key words and phrases are then introduced before students watch the main video section, which includes a number of short videos on different aspects of the topic. Here, students can develop listening and note-taking skills with language presented in an authentic context. Each lesson ends with activities to give students speaking practice on the topics in the videos.

About Saïd Business School

Saïd Business School is part of the University of Oxford. It blends the best of new and old – it is a vibrant and innovative business school, yet deeply embedded in an 800-year-old world-class university. Saïd Business School creates programmes and ideas that have global impact – it educates people for successful business careers and, as a community, seeks to tackle world-scale problems. The school delivers cutting-edge programmes and ground-breaking research that transform individuals, organizations, business practice and society. Find out more at www.sbs.ox.ac.uk

Additional material

The following sections are in the back of the *Student's Book*.

Practice files

These provide unit-by-unit support for your classroom work. Each file provides additional practice of target language from the *Working with words*, *Business communication* and *Language at work* sections of each unit. This can be used in two ways:

For extra practice in class – refer students to this section for more controlled practice of new vocabulary, grammar or key expressions before moving to the next stage. The optimum point at which to do this is indicated by cross references in the *Student's Book* unit and the teaching notes in this book.

For self-study – students can complete and self-check the exercises for review and revision outside class.

Answers for the *Practice file* exercises appear on pages 93–96 of this *Teacher's Book*.

Communication activities

Additional information for pairwork and group activities.

Audio scripts

Irregular verb list

TEACHER'S BOOK

What's in each unit?

Unit content

This provides an overview of the main aims and objectives of the unit.

Context

This section not only provides information on the teaching points covered in the unit, but also offers some background information on the main business theme of the unit and its importance in the current business world. If you are less familiar with the world of business, you will find this section especially helpful to read before starting a unit.

Teaching notes and answers

Notes on managing the *Student's Book* exercises and various activities are given throughout, with suggested variations that you might like to try. You will find comprehensive answers to all *Student's Book* exercises, as well as notes on possible responses to discussion questions.

One-to-one

In general, you will find that *Business Result Second Edition* can be used with any size of class. However, with one-to-one students, activities which have been designed for groups of students will need some adaptation. The *Teacher's Book* provides suggestions for how to adapt group work activities successfully for one-to-one classes.

Pre-work learners

Although most users of *Business Result Second Edition* will be students who are already in work, you may also be teaching classes of students who have little or no experience of the business world. The *Teacher's Book* provides suggestions for how to adapt certain questions or tasks in the book to their needs, and extra notes are given for these types of learners.

Extension

With some students it may be appropriate to extend an exercise in some way or relate the language point more specifically to a particular group of students. Suggestions on how to do this are given where appropriate.

Extra activity

If you have time or would like to develop further areas of language competence, extra activities are suggested where they naturally follow the order of activities in the *Student's Book*. For example, if your students need writing practice or need to build more confidence with speaking, extra follow-up ideas may be provided for those aspects.

Alternative

With some students it may be preferable to approach an activity in a different way, depending on their level or their interests. These options are provided where appropriate.

Pronunciation

Tips on teaching pronunciation and helping students improve their intelligibility are provided where there is a logical need for them. These often appear where new vocabulary is taught, or where making key expressions sound more natural and fluent is important.

Dictionary skills

It's helpful to encourage students to use a good dictionary in class and the teaching notes suggest moments in the lesson when it may be useful to develop your students' skills in using dictionaries.

USING THE COURSE

How to use *Business Result Second Edition* to fit your teaching context

Business Result Second Edition provides all the flexibility you need as a teacher. The syllabus and content has been carefully designed so that it can be used either from start to finish, or in a modular way, allowing you to tailor the course to suit your and your students' needs.

Using the course from start to finish

You can, of course, use *Business Result Second Edition* conventionally, starting at *Unit 1* and working your way through each unit in turn. If you do so, you will find it works well. Each section of the unit is related thematically to the others, and there is a degree of recycling and a steady progression towards overall competence, culminating in the *Talking point* or *Viewpoint*. Timing will inevitably vary, but allow approximately four classroom hours for each unit. You will need more time if you intend to do the *Practice file* activities in class.

The 'flexible' option

Business Result Second Edition is written in a way that recognizes that many business English courses vary greatly in length. With this in mind, teachers can use *Business Result Second Edition* in a modular way. Although each unit has a logical progression, you will find that all the sections are essentially free-standing and can be used independently of the rest of the unit.

This modular approach provides the flexibility that business English teachers need when planning their course. Teachers might want to choose the sections or unit topics that are the most relevant and interesting to them and their students.

Online practice and teacher resources

For students

The *Online practice* gives your students additional language practice of the *Student's Book* content. For more information, see page 5 of the *Student's Book*.

For teachers

As well as providing access to all of the student online practice exercises, the Learning Management System (LMS) is an invaluable and time-saving tool for teachers.

You can monitor your students' progress and all of their results at the touch of a button. You can also print off and use student reports on their progress.

A training guide for how to use the LMS can be found in the *Guides* section of the *Online practice*.

Downloadable resources for teachers

The teacher resources in the *Online practice* include the following downloadable resources for teachers to use to complement the *Student's Book*:

• Photocopiable worksheets for every unit
• Progress tests for every unit
• Business cards for role-plays
• Class audio
• Class video

Photocopiable worksheets

New for *Business Result Second Edition* are the photocopiable worksheets. These provide extra communicative practice, often in the form of a game, for every *Working with words*, *Business communication* and *Language at work* section in the *Student's Book*.

There are suggestions in the *Teacher's Book* for when to use these worksheets in class. All of the worksheets, as well as the answer key, can be downloaded and photocopied from the teacher resources in the *Online practice*.

Photocopiable Progress tests

These can be administered at the end of each unit in order to assess your students' progress and allow you, the students or the head of training to keep track of students' overall ability.

Each test is divided into two sections. The first section tests the vocabulary, grammar and key expressions from the unit. This section is scored out of 30 and students will need about 30 minutes to complete the questions.

The second section is a speaking test. In this section students are given a speaking task that resembles one of the speaking activities in the unit. These are mostly set up as pairwork activities in the form of role-plays, discussions or presentations.

Marking criteria is provided to help you assess students' performance in the speaking test. It requires students to perform five functions in the speaking test, and you can grade each of the five stages using a scoring system of 0, 1 or 2, giving a final score out of 10.

The speaking test role-plays can also be used as extra classroom practice without necessarily making use of the marking criteria.

All of the tests, and the answer keys, can be downloaded from the teacher resources in the *Online practice*.

Business cards

There is a set of downloadable business cards in the teacher resources in the *Online practice*.

The business cards are particularly useful to use in role-play situations from the *Student's Book* if you have students from the same company and they are required to exchange information about their company.

Class audio and video

All of the class audio and the videos for the *Viewpoint* lessons can be streamed or downloaded from the teacher resources in the *Online practice*. Students also have access to the class audio and video in their version of the *Online practice*.

Alternatively, class audio can be played from the audio CD and the videos can be played from the DVD that is found in the *Teacher's Book* pack.

How to access the *Online practice*

For students

Students should use the access card on the inside front cover of the *Student's Book*. This contains an access code to unlock the content in the *Online practice*.

For teachers

Teachers need to go to **www.oxfordlearn.com** and either register or sign in. If you are registered with the Oxford Teachers' Club, Oxford Learner's Bookshelf or Oxford Learner's Dictionaries, you can use your existing username and password to sign in.

Then click on **Register an organization** and follow the instructions. Note that if you are not part of an organization, or you don't have an authorization code from your institution, you will need to click on **Apply for an organization account**. You will then be asked to supply some information. If you don't have an institution, then put your own name next to Institution name.

Teacher's website

Additional teacher resources can be found at **www.oup.com/elt/teacher/businessresult**

Unit content

By the end of this unit, students will be able to
- talk about first impressions
- arrange to meet and exchange contact details
- talk about work routines, projects and plans using the present simple and present continuous.

Context

The topic of *First impressions* will relate to your students not only at an individual level, when one person meets another, but also at a company level, where a client gets an impression of the whole company.

Companies use many 'instruments' for presenting a certain image, which are both tangible and intangible. The tangible physical factors include such things as business cards, publicity materials, their premises and of course social media (e.g. Facebook, Twitter, etc.). All these will affect our view of the business. In addition, there are the intangible factors such as professionalism and reputation, and the warmth of our welcome in reception. Many of your students may even be learning English as part of the company's need for staff to be able to communicate confidently with overseas visitors and give a good impression.

With international settings, first impressions are also affected by cultural differences; the impression one nationality or culture gains can be different to another, so it's wise for a company to be culturally aware of the messages it is giving.

The first part of this unit opens up the discussion of giving good first impressions, including the need for individuals to be aware of their own online profile, and the issues of adapting websites to meet the needs of different local cultures. Students then practise the necessary communication skills of meeting people for the first time and networking. In the *Talking point*, students discuss the overlap between our working life and personal life.

If you are starting this unit on a new course with new students, you might want to exploit the context for students to get to know their peers. You can encourage students to work with different people in the classroom so as to achieve a sense of 'team spirit' and collaboration as quickly as possible.

Starting point

Discuss these two questions as a class. You could adapt or extend question 2 by asking students to think of five words that describe the impression they think visitors and clients have of their own company. You could also ask students how important they think the following are for first impressions:

- atmosphere of company/building
- relationship between colleagues and/or management and staff
- customer service
- company values

EXTENSION Ask students: *Do you give a different impression when speaking a foreign language?* This is a good moment, if it is the beginning of the course, to get students talking about how they use English and why it is important. Find out if they need English to improve the image of their company.

PRE-WORK LEARNERS Students could consider what impressions they and others have of their school or college. Discuss what image the college brochures, building and its website give.

Working with words

Exercise 1

Ask students to read the question, and share their ideas with the class. Encourage them to come up with as many ideas as possible.

Possible answers
online, on social media, through talking to other people

Exercise 2

Students read the text and decide which brief summary, a–c, matches each paragraph.

Answers
a 2 **b** 1 **c** 3

Exercise 3

Students read the questions and then underline the answers in the text. They can then compare answers in pairs. Check students understand *to track* (*eye movements*) and *to gain* (*their first impression*).

Answers
1 (paragraph 1) '… searched your name, checked to see if your company has a good reputation via online review sites and even searched your personal online history.'
2 (paragraph 2) '… the logo, photographs, menus and, in particular, the opportunity to make contact via social media.'
3 (paragraph 3) '… finding out that the information on the CV didn't match the applicant's online profile.' / '… make sure their online profile promotes a positive and truthful image.'

PRONUNCIATION Ask students to identify how many syllables there are in the words below from **3** and to mark the word stress. Drill the words as necessary.

Answers
impression (3), prospective (3), potential (3), guarantee (3), reputation (4), researcher (3) (researcher is also accepted), opportunity (5), individual (5), freelancer (3), employer (3), employee (3), rejection (3)

Exercise 4

Students read the questions, and then complete them using one of the words in italics. Students can refer to the text to check their answers. Draw students' attention to the fact that the words in all the phrases are common verb + noun combinations, except number 6, which is a phrasal verb.

Answers

1	create	**5**	form
2	have	**6**	come
3	project	**7**	build
4	manage	**8**	take

Exercise 5

Students work in pairs and take turns to ask and answer five of the questions in **4**.

If this is the first lesson with a new class, don't assume all students will be familiar with working in pairs. You may need to set it up carefully and even explain the rationale.

PRE-WORK LEARNERS For questions 1, 2, 3 and 7, use these alternatives:

1 What kind of impression do you think your college (or a business you know well) likes to create on its website?

2 What sort of reputation do you think your college has?

3 Imagine seeing brochures and advertising for your college for the first time: what sort of image do they project? Does this match your own impressions and experience?

7 Consider your experience as a customer of a business you know well, or use regularly. What has the company done to help to build a close relationship with you? How have you / has the company benefited?

Exercise 6

ALTERNATIVE ▶ 1.1 In **6**, students need to listen and make notes on quite a lengthy listening. If students aren't confident with listening at this early stage of the course, write the following questions on the board and play the listening once. Students only need to listen for short answers (shown in brackets).

1 *Which markets do Western companies want to break into?* (Asian)

2 *What do these companies want Zhifu's help with?* (websites)

3 *Is it enough to translate a site?* (no)

4 *What is important to understand when designing a website?* (local culture)

5 *Where should you start the process of making a website for the Asian consumer?* (from the beginning)

▶ **1.1** Ask students to read the two questions before listening. If some of your students have international experience with websites or advertising, ask them to comment on what they think the answers might be before they listen.

Answers
1 Zhifu says that, as in traditional advertising, some things are more effective in some cultures than others.
2 Websites for Western consumers have lots of words and facts, and are often quite complex. Websites for Asian consumers tend to be more simple, functional and less ostentatious. Asian consumers also prefer sites where you can bargain.

Exercise 7

Students match the adjectives.

Answers

1	reliable: trustworthy	**7**	practical: functional
2	unsuccessful: ineffective	**8**	complicated: complex
3	showy: ostentatious	**9**	simple: modest
4	positive: favourable	**10**	effective: successful
5	costly: expensive	**11**	over-confident: arrogant
6	mistrustful: suspicious	**12**	cautious: wary

DICTIONARY SKILLS
Students will find it helpful to use dictionaries for the task in **7**. If up to this level, your students have only used bilingual dictionaries, this may be a good moment to introduce them to monolingual dictionaries and show how they can be used for checking words and word stress. As an extra task, ask students to underline the word stress in each word. Drill these words as necessary.

Exercise 8

Students do the activity in pairs. Some of the answers for question 1 are quite clear. For example, *reliable* is universally a positive adjective. However, being *cautious* can be both positive and negative depending on the context and possibly the culture. Where students don't agree, discuss the word and its different uses, and try to elicit or give examples.

When students discuss questions 2 and 3, it may be helpful to have examples of websites to refer to. If you have access to computers in the classroom, students could show each other different websites.

Possible answers
1 positive: reliable, trustworthy, positive, favourable, practical, functional, simple, effective, successful
negative: ostentatious, unsuccessful, ineffective, showy, costly, expensive, mistrustful, suspicious, over-confident, arrogant
potentially both positive and negative: complicated, complex, modest, cautious, wary

EXTENSION Students who work for companies with websites or study at colleges with a site could assess the websites with their partner.

Further practice

If students need more practice, go to *Practice file 1* on page 106 of the *Student's Book*.

Exercise 9

After students have worked through each of the tasks, they can present their views and ideas to the rest of the class.

PRE-WORK LEARNERS Most of the criteria in **9** will apply when discussing a place of study, so students should be able to discuss these with reference to their school or college.

Photocopiable worksheet

Download and photocopy *Unit 1 Working with words* worksheet from the teacher resources in the *Online practice*.

Business communication

Exercise 1

Students read the questions and discuss their answers and ideas with a partner. Elicit some of their answers to find out if there are any similarities in the kinds of meetings they have or arrange.

PRE-WORK LEARNERS Students can think of a situation in their private life or related to their studies when they have to meet up with others, and answer the questions.

Exercise 2

Ask students to look at the email to Mr McFee and say how formal it is. In terms of formality, how similar is it to the emails they send and receive? Note that emails can be seen as less formal than letters, but the register here is normal for day-to-day business.

Students read the email and can compare their answers for 1–3 with a partner.

Answers
1 from Sean's former colleague
2 to ask for help with the renewal/design of a website
3 call or email to arrange a meeting

Exercise 3

▶ **1.2** Students listen and answer the questions.

Answers
1 It's a follow-up call to the email Sean sent to Ivan.
2 They arrange to meet to discuss things further.
3 Ivan is going to be in Berlin the day after tomorrow.

Exercise 4

▶ **1.2** Students can work alone to order the sentences, and listen again to check their answers.

Explain the meaning of *provisionally* (= arranged for the present time, but it might change).

You could refer students to the *Tip* and use of *actually* here and compare it with *currently* (from listening 1.2).

Answers
a 2 b 1 c 3 d 7 e 9 f 10 g 4 h 5 i 6 j 8

Exercise 5

▶ **1.3** Students listen and answer the questions.

Answers
1 Catherine, Ivan Formanek's assistant, is calling to confirm the meeting on the 13th.
2 She will email a map and directions.
3 public transport

Exercise 6

▶ **1.3** Students listen again and make a note of the phrases used.

Answers
1 a Can you tell me how I get to Simply Speaking? Is it best by taxi or public transport?
  b There's a train that leaves at three o'clock.
  c Will I have time to catch that one (or should I take a later one)?
2 a Let me know where you're staying and I'll email you a map and directions from your hotel.
  b Let me know if you need a taxi and I'll book one for you.

ALTERNATIVE If your students find it hard to listen and make a note of phrases at the same time, suggest they find and underline the phrases in the audio script on page 140 of the *Student's Book* or tick the phrases they hear in the *Key expressions*.

Further practice

If students need more practice, go to *Practice file 1* on page 106 of the *Student's Book*.

Exercise 7

Draw students' attention to the first section of the *Key expressions*. These will be useful for writing their emails.

Students work alone and prepare their email. Ask them to write the email on a piece of paper rather than in a notebook as they will exchange emails with a partner.

PRE-WORK LEARNERS Students can think of a scenario in their private life or related to their studies. However, if they need help, suggest they imagine they work for a corporate training company. They write an email to a prospective client who might be interested in courses on presentation skills.

Exercise 8

To help students to structure their calls, talk through each stage and elicit possible phrases to use. Make sure they are aware they can use the *Key expressions* to help.

Give feedback on use of the phrases and how students structured their calls. At the end, students can comment on their calls and say where they felt they had particular difficulty or success.

PRONUNCIATION If your students regularly make phone calls in English, encourage them to think about how to say the phone phrases, focusing on stressing key words and sounding friendly.

You could ask them to choose two or three phrases from each category in the *Key expressions* they would like to use, and to do the following:
– underline the important words / words they would stress
– ask them to think about whether their intonation should go up or down if they want to sound friendly and polite, e.g. start high, middle or low; end high or low, e.g.

I was given your details by XY. The intonation starts in the middle, is a bit higher on details, and falls at the end of the sentence.

When would you like to meet? The intonation starts high and falls on *meet*.

Can you tell me how I get to … XY? The intonation starts high and falls at the end.

Do one together first.

Students then compare the phrases they have picked with a partner and practise saying each one out loud.

Photocopiable worksheet
Download and photocopy *Unit 1 Business communication* worksheet from the teacher resources in the *Online practice*.

Practically speaking

Exercise 1
Students read the questions and share their answers and ideas with a partner. Ask them to consider both professional and personal contexts. Elicit a few ideas from the class.

Exercise 2
▶ **1.4** Students listen and answer the questions.

> **Answers**
> Conversation 1: 1 business card 2 about the next exhibition
> Conversation 2: 1 text 2 to invite Suzy
> Conversation 3: 1 email 2 to get together again

Exercise 3
▶ **1.4** Students listen again and match the phrases to the calls.

> **Answers**
> 2 Call 3   5 Call 3
> 3 Call 2   6 Call 1
> 4 Call 2

Exercise 4
Students put the phrases from **3** into three categories.

> **Answers**
> a 1, 2, 4   b 6   c 3, 5

Exercise 5
If students still don't know everyone in the class, they can use their own identity and details in this activity. However, you could also ask students to make notes on a new identity. They write a name, a number and an email address. They could even prepare home numbers and email addresses as well as those for work. As an alternative, in groups of four, they could talk in pairs and then change partners to give the contact details of the other person they were talking to. Elicit or remind students how to say @ (at), as well as how to say phone numbers: in English, we say numbers separately, except for 'double' numbers, e.g. 0208-579-6646: *oh two oh eight, five seven nine, double six four six.*

ONE-TO-ONE Take in some business cards you have, or invent some and put them on small pieces of card. (Avoid any which have a direct or real connection with your student's work). In class, take a card each in turn and exchange contact details.

Language at work

Exercise 1
Students read the sentences and discuss in pairs which tense is used, and why. Do the first one together as an example.
Note that discussion on why each tense is used will be given in **2**.

> **Answers**
> Present simple = b, d, e, g, h
> Present continuous = a, c, f, i

Exercise 2
Students answer the questions in the *Language point*. Students can compare answers in pairs.

> **Answers**
> 1 d 2 e 3 b 4 g 5 h 6 a 7 c 8 f 9 i

Grammar reference
If students need more information, go to *Grammar reference* on page 107 of the *Student's Book*.

Exercise 3
Students prepare questions for each of the areas. Make sure they use a variety of present simple and present continuous forms. Do the first one together.

> **Possible questions**
> Who do you work for?
> Which department do you work in?
> What are you responsible for?
> What are you working on at the moment?
> What's your typical day? / What do you do each day?
> How often do you need to use English at work?
> How are your English studies going?
> What are you doing next week at work?

PRE-WORK LEARNERS Students could replace work-related issues with those related to their studies, e.g. where they are studying, the area of their studies, etc.

Exercise 4

Students take turns to ask and answer the questions in **3**. The focus here should be on accuracy with the tenses, both in terms of the questions asked and the responses.

Exercise 5

Note that this question asks students to say which phrases they would normally expect to appear with the tenses. It's feasible that all of them could appear with the present simple or a range of other tenses including the future, conditionals, past tense, etc.

> **Answers**
> present simple: generally speaking, on the whole, once a week, most of the time, every winter, once in a while, as a rule
> present continuous: for the moment, at the moment, for the time being, tomorrow afternoon, right now, currently

Exercise 6

You might like to give a few examples from your own life to illustrate the activity. For example: *I'm teaching here at the moment. / Once a week I go to the cinema.*

PRE-WORK LEARNERS Ask students to use the phrases to talk about their studies.

> **Further practice**
> If students need more practice, go to *Practice file 1* on page 107 of the *Student's Book*.

Exercise 7

This activity gives students a chance to finally get to know everyone in the class and find out about each other's companies. Students will need a little time to prepare and then the presentations can be given to the rest of the class. Set a time limit of 1–2 minutes for each talk. At the end, if a presenter hasn't mentioned all the points listed, other students can ask questions to find out the answers or anything else they would like to know about the speaker.

If students are from the same company, they could give a presentation about their department. Otherwise, they will probably still be interested to hear what features of the company each person highlights. Listen and make notes on any problems with the tenses used. Write any problematic sentences on the board and discuss and correct them.

PRE-WORK LEARNERS Students could talk about a company they know well and like, and prepare this at home for next time.

> **Photocopiable worksheet**
> Download and photocopy *Unit 1 Language at work* worksheet from the teacher resources in the *Online practice*.

Talking point

Discussion

Exercise 1

Before students read the text, you could ask them, with books closed, to think about their work and personal lives, and if there is a clear distinction between the two or not.

Write the following questions on the board:

1 *What can happen if someone's work and personal lives are very separate?* (They may be frustrated.)
2 *Why is it better if work and personal lives overlap?* (They are probably working on things which interest them.)

Then ask students to open their books and read the information. They should also look at the diagrams on work-life overlap. Ask students to read the question in **1** and share their answers and ideas with a partner.

PRE-WORK LEARNERS For this exercise and the ones that follow, ask students to think about their studies and personal life.

Exercise 2

Students discuss with a partner how easy they find it to separate their work and non-work life.

Exercise 3

Ask students to give reasons and examples for their answer(s). Elicit a few ideas from the class.

Task

Exercise 1

Students draw two circles to represent their own work and personal life. They then work with a partner to explain their circles and any overlap.

Exercise 2

You could put students with a new partner for this exercise. Students complete the blank Venn diagram to represent what they and their partner have in common. Make notes on how well they ask for and share information about themselves. Give them feedback on this at the end of the activity.

Remind students of the word order: *both* comes before the main verb, but after the verb *to be*.

EXTENSION Depending on how well your students know each other, you could ask students to work with another pair and clarify what they have in common. See if they can find out anything the two pairs (i.e. four students) have in common.

Alternatively, some pairs of students could present their diagrams to the class. Encourage other students to ask questions.

> **Progress test**
> Download and photocopy *Unit 1 Progress test* and *Speaking test* from the teacher resources in the *Online practice*.

2 Motivation

Unit content

By the end of this unit, students will be able to

• talk about motivation

• encourage and end conversations politely

• use different questions to check information or start conversations.

Context

The topic of *Motivation* may apply to your students in different ways. For management, the issue is how to make staff work more effectively and find ways of ensuring they continue to give 100%. For staff, motivation may be a question of how much they are paid or what the perks and benefits of a job are.

However, what motivates us is more complex than simply money or bonuses. Psychologist and business management theorist Frederick Herzberg discovered that factors such as working conditions, salary, status and job security do not necessarily lead to higher levels of motivation, although without them there will be dissatisfaction. In fact, achievement, recognition, career advancement, job interest and satisfaction are the factors which will bring about staff motivation.

Since Herzberg's famous article on his findings 'One More Time, How Do You Motivate Employees?', other studies show that motivation is also affected by an employee's cultural background. For example, a recent study of motivation with Chinese workers showed that personal loyalty from the manager and organization was rated more highly than how interesting the work itself was. This was especially true of older workers. If you have a mixed-nationality class, this is perhaps an area you could explore and discuss.

While the first part of this unit deals with the language students will need to discuss motivation, the unit also prepares them for encouraging conversation in social situations. To support this communication skill, there is a review of question forms within a social context. When students reach the *Talking point*, they will discuss the language companies use to motivate their customers.

Starting point

Discuss the two questions as a class, or students can work in pairs or small groups to decide what motivates them and what else could be added to the list. Some other possible things to add include: bonuses, a company car, a pension, praise, travel, holidays, a good boss.

PRE-WORK LEARNERS Ask students what motivates them to study for their current qualification or what motivates them to learn English, e.g. *If I can speak English, I'll get a better job with better pay and perhaps have the chance to travel …*

EXTENSION Ask the class to do the following:

1 Put the list of things in question 1 in order of importance from 1 to 8 (1= most important, 8 = least important).

2 Compare your results with the rest of the class.

Working with words

Exercise 1

Allow time for students to think about their answers to these questions and then discuss as a class. Find out about any internships or work experience your students have taken part in, and how they benefited.

Exercise 2

Before reading, check students understand *internship* – a short period when a student or recent graduate works at a company to gain experience.

Students read the questions and then find the answers in the text. Alternatively, you could ask students to read and discuss the questions for two minutes with a partner, and then compare their answers with the information in the text.

Answers
to take their first step on the career ladder
get hands-on work experience
show a future employer you are motivated
learn about the professional work environment
meet future contacts
make a difference at your first job interview

Exercise 3

Students read the statements and then read the text again to decide if they are true or false. Students can compare answers in pairs.

Answers
1 F (many global companies offer internship programmes)
2 T (the majority do not come with a cash reward)
3 F (it may lead to a full-time position later on)
4 T (menial tasks)
5 T (let the company know your areas of interest)
6 T (this could make all the difference at your first interview for a paid job)

After you have checked the answers, check the meaning of *menial* (not skilled or important, and often boring and badly paid).

Exercise 4

Students match each word in each pair with a definition.

Answers
1 enthusiasm b / self-motivation a
2 reward a / incentive b
3 achievement a / performance b
4 benefit a / appreciate b
5 praise b / recognition a

PRONUNCIATION Check students know where each word is stressed (see underlining in Answers above), and also that they can say the underlined sounds in these words correctly: enthusiasm /ɪnˈθjuːziæzəm/, appreciate /əˈpriːʃieɪt/, recognition /ˌrekəgˈnɪʃn/. If necessary, show them how you make the sound.

Exercise 5

Students work in pairs and ask and answer the two questions. Elicit a few ideas to share with the class.

PRE-WORK LEARNERS Ask students to reflect on the words in **4** in light of their own work or study experience, e.g. how much self-motivation they have, and for what kind of work/ tasks; how they or others measure their own achievements or performance; what sort of praise and/or recognition they have received and the effect it has on their work/studies.

Exercise 6

▶ **2.1** Draw the table frame from Answers below on the board for students to copy. When they listen, they can use it to make notes and you can write their answers on the board.

Answers

		Claudia	Peter	Macie
1	Job	sales rep selling soap, shampoo and toiletries	manager of a car dealership	flight attendant
2	Benefits, rewards, incentives	BlackBerry and laptop, company car, commission of 15%, merchandise, vouchers, social events	sales competition with prizes, reward vouchers (hot-air balloon trip, spa treatment), special trips, training/staff development, staff discount	reduced fares for the family, compensation plan (profit-sharing scheme, non-contributory pension plan, medical insurance), attendance rewards, on-time bonuses
3	Other factors	meeting new people, travel, autonomy, being acknowledged and recognized for achievements	positive feedback, praise	travel and seeing different countries on long-haul flights, senior management comes round and thanks staff personally

Exercise 7

Before starting, check students understand the difference between *material* and *non-material benefits*: *material* = you can see/touch them (e.g. money, possessions); *non-material* = you can't see/touch them (e.g. good feelings).

Answers
Material benefits: company car, commission, staff discount, attendance reward, on-time bonus, compensation plan, private medical insurance, non-contributory pension plan
Non-material benefits: autonomy, feel valued, be acknowledged, appreciation, positive feedback, (personal) development, praise, satisfaction, (sense of) achievement

DICTIONARY SKILLS
There are a number of words/phrases in this list or in the listening that may cause students difficulty, so they will find it useful to use a dictionary. As a starting point, ask them to look up the following words and identify what type of word they are (adjective or noun): *commission* (noun), *compensation* (noun), *contributory* (adjective), *fulfilment* (noun), *autonomy* (noun), *acknowledged* (adjective).
You could also ask students to find other forms of the words, e.g. verbs: *to compensate, to contribute, to fulfil, to acknowledge.*

PRONUNCIATION Students can also check which syllable is stressed in these words.

Answers
commission, compensation, contributory, fulfilment, autonomy, acknowledged

Exercise 8

Be aware, when you set up this activity, that if your class contains employees from the same company with different employment contracts, some students may feel uncomfortable about discussing contracts. Remind students that they should discuss only what the norm in their own countries is and not be specific about details.

PRE-WORK LEARNERS If your students are unable to answer these questions from experience, you could ask them to find out after class, by speaking to a friend or relative, and report back next time. Alternatively, they should be able to discuss question 3 with reference to their future choice of career.

Further practice

If students need more practice, go to *Practice file 2* on page 108 of the *Student's Book*.

Exercise 9

Allow about 15–20 minutes to complete this activity. Make sure groups nominate someone to take notes on their ideas so that they can present them to the class at the end.

As you listen to the discussion or the presentation of each group's decisions at the end, make notes on any incorrect usage or pronunciation of the vocabulary in the section. Set aside a few minutes afterwards to draw attention to meaning or use, and drill any difficult pronunciation.

ONE-TO-ONE You could decide together on the type of company. You could then work individually on question 2, and then swap ideas to work on each other's suggestions for question 3. Then discuss your ideas and work on question 4 together.

Photocopiable worksheet

Download and photocopy *Unit 2 Working with words* worksheet from the teacher resources in the *Online practice*.

Business communication

Exercise 1

Students read the questions and share their ideas. You could start by eliciting one idea for each question first.

Exercise 2

Students read the text and try to reach a final agreement on which five tips are the most useful. With a mixed-nationality class, this activity should raise many cultural issues relating to what is/isn't appropriate when making small talk. For example, tip 1 suggests that using first names (*Hi, I'm Jules…*) is acceptable. In some cultures, this may not be the case.

Exercise 3

▶ **2.2** Students read the *Context* and the two questions for each conversation. Then play the listening.

Answers
Conversation 1
1 The first speaker uses a number of the tips including 1 and 3.
2 The conversation fails because the second speaker answers briefly and makes no effort to develop the conversation (tip 6).
Conversation 2
1 Both speakers follow a number of the tips including 2 (repeating names) and 5 (flowing conversation).
2 The conversation is successful because of this.
Conversation 3
1 This conversation is a good example of two people finding a shared experience (tip 4) and tips 1, 5 and 6 are used.
2 The conversation is successful because of this.
Conversation 4
1 Adam quickly starts describing problems (tip 8).
2 The conversation is unsuccessful because of this and Adriana quickly uses an exit strategy.

Exercise 4

▶ **2.2** Allow time for students to read questions 1–7 before listening again. Note that listening and writing out phrases can take time, so students may need to hear the conversations more than once.

Answers
1 Hello, I saw you … but I didn't have a chance to speak to you. I'm Harry.
2 Well, it's been nice talking to you. / You don't mind if I go and get myself a coffee? / See you later.
3 Hi, I don't think we've met. I'm Paolo from …
4 Hi, nice to meet you. I'm Sonia from …
5 That's amazing! / What a coincidence!
6 Good evening … / How lovely to see you here.
7 She responds by saying: Oh dear. / Oh, I'm so sorry to hear that.

EXTRA ACTIVITY
▶ **2.2** Play the listening again and ask students to write down any more phrases (other than those in **4**) they think are useful for making small talk. Alternatively, ask them to underline the phrases in the audio script on page 141 of the *Student's Book*.

Possible answers
Start a conversation
Conversation 3: I'm … , based in ….
Conversation 4: I thought I might see you.
Finish a conversation
Conversation 4: Look, I have to go. Catch you later.
Keep the conversation going
Conversation 1: Would you like another drink?
Conversation 2: I've heard that … – is that true?
Conversation 3: Isn't it famous for …?
Conversation 3: So have you spent much time … recently?
Leave a conversation
Conversation 1: You don't mind if I go and get myself a coffee? See you later.

Exercise 5

▶ **2.3** Students listen out for and number the phrases. Discuss how these phrases help the conversation flow. Note that some show interest or surprise (*What a coincidence! / Really?*), some are asking questions (*Don't you … / … by the way?*) and others link information and ideas (*So … / In fact … / Apparently …*). Encourage students also to listen out for how the phrases are said, including where the phrases are stressed, and if the intonation goes up or down after the stressed part.

Answers
a 5 **b** 1 **c** 3 **d** 4 **e** 6 **f** 9 **g** 2 **h** 8 **i** 10 **j** 7

Refer students to the *Tip* on *well* and *so* on page 14 of the *Student's Book*. To illustrate how these words are used, you could play listening **2.3** again as the speakers use them.

Further practice

If students need more practice, go to *Practice file 2* on page 108 of the *Student's Book*.

Exercise 6

Students work on improving conversations 1 and 4 which are unsuccessful. Refer students to the *Key expressions* and ask them to think about which phrases they could use.

Possible answers

2   In conversation 1, Alessandro only uses short answers and doesn't try to extend the conversation. One way to solve this would be to give extra information, ask questions and show interest. In conversation 4, Adam goes into too much detail about problems and doesn't ask anything about Adriana.

You could play conversations 2 and 3 again for students to focus specifically on the phrases they highlighted in **5**, and which they'll need to improve conversations 1 and 4.

Exercise 7

This is free practice, with students starting and maintaining a conversation. Remind them to refer to the *Key expressions*. To add realism to the task, ask students to stand up, as if at a conference. With large classes, you could suggest that when students feel they have finished a conversation with one partner, they should use an exit strategy to end the conversation and move on to another person.

Give feedback on phrases used during the conversation. If you have video equipment, you could record the students' conversations and afterwards comment on appropriate body language as well as conversation content. If students have difficulty with exit strategies, note that this skill is dealt with in *Practically speaking*.

Photocopiable worksheet

Download and photocopy *Unit 2 Business communication* worksheet from the teacher resources in the *Online practice*.

Practically speaking

Exercise 1

▶ **2.4** Allow time for students to try to match the two parts of the phrases 1–5 to a–e. Then play the listening for students to check.

You could also elicit any other suitable excuses they think would be appropriate.

Answers

1 b   2 e   3 c   4 d   5 a

Remind students that *how* they say something can be more important than the words they use. Model the sentences, focusing on sentence stress and intonation, or use the audio. Get students to repeat.

Exercise 2

Students look at the four situations. Before role-playing the situations, ask them to discuss which phrases are appropriate to use in each case, and then try using them at the end of their small talk.

Alternatively, you could put the five phrases for ending a conversation, or just a cue word from each phrase, on strips of paper and ask students to use a different one for each conversation, together with an appropriate excuse.

Listen in, and afterwards give feedback on use of phrases.

Language at work

Exercise 1

Students read the questions and decide which ones they would use with someone they think they might know.

Students will find it useful to refer to the *Tip* on question use here. You could ask them to suggest some example questions for each use.

Answers

a, f

Exercise 2

Students read the *Language point* and first match the example questions from **1** to the three categories. Then ask them to answer the five questions.

Answers

Indirect questions: b, e
1   I'd like to know / Can you tell me
2   after the subject
Negative questions: c, d
3   the contracted form
Question tags: a, f
4   'Yes' (affirmative)
5   negative

Grammar reference

If students need more information, go to *Grammar reference* on page 109 of the *Student's Book*.

Exercise 3

Students work in pairs to rewrite the questions using the prompts provided. They can compare them with the rest of the class, before asking and answering the questions.

Possible answers

2   how much the room is per night
3   you with Unilever for a few years
4   where you buy your packaging from
5   don't I
6   what time the exhibition hall opens
7   don't you meet us
8   said they'd join us, didn't they

Further practice

If students need more practice, go to *Practice file 2* on page 109 of the *Student's Book*.

PRONUNCIATION   Note that we often use question tags to check and confirm. In this case, the intonation will fall:
That wasn't a very interesting presentation, was it?
However, if rising intonation is used over the tag, this indicates the speaker is less certain of what the answer is, i.e. it's more of a real question:
The meeting won't finish late, will it?
You can also use the same sentence to demonstrate this, first with falling intonation on the tag (getting confirmation), and then with rising intonation (as a real question), e.g.
The lesson finishes today at 5, doesn't it?
Drill sentences 1–8 in **3** with their tags and practise the falling intonation, and then drill again with rising intonation.

Exercise 4

Students read the situations and think of two questions they could ask in each one. Then put students in pairs and ask them to role-play the situations. You could ask them to role-play two situations and then change pairs and role-play two more situations (the same or different) with their new partner.

If you have an odd number of students, or can make groups of three, you could ask the extra or third student to listen in and note down, for each person, how many questions of each type they ask, e.g. Ivan: indirect questions – 2; question tags – 1.

Listen to their conversations and make a note on their use of questions. Then be ready to give feedback on accurate use of questions (word order, positive and negative auxiliaries and intonation).

> **EXTRA ACTIVITY**
> Ask students to write down a different question type to ask three different people in the class: one indirect question, one negative question and one question tag question, paying close attention to word order and positive and negative auxiliaries. When they are ready, ask students to stand and mingle around the class, finding each person, asking them their question and noting the answer. Students then return to their seats. Ask students to report back to the class on anything interesting they found out from the other students.

Photocopiable worksheet

Download and photocopy *Unit 2 Language at work* worksheet from the teacher resources in the *Online practice*.

Talking point

Discussion

Exercise 1

Before students read the text, ask them to read the question and discuss their ideas and answers with a partner. Encourage them to say what it is specifically that motivates them to buy products or services based on adverts or social media, e.g. the picture, the words, or something else. Try to elicit a few specific examples.

Students read the text. Ask them to compare their ideas; did they mention any of the words listed?

Exercise 2

Students consider their own company's advertising, and whether they use any of the words listed or similar words. You could ask them how effective they think they are.

PRE-WORK LEARNERS Suggest students think about a company they know well (local or international) and to consider some of its advertising and the strategies it uses. Can they remember any of the words listed appearing in the company's advertising?

Exercise 3

Ask students to focus on the final paragraph, and the words in italics, and elicit their ideas for why these might be demotivating. Encourage them to share their ideas about the use of capital letters.

Task

Exercise 1

Students first work alone to think of words about their product or service which would motivate customers. Then ask them to explain their choices to a partner.

PRE-WORK LEARNERS Suggest students work in pairs and choose a product or service they both know to work with. They could then join with another pair to share their five words.

ONE-TO-ONE Your student could choose their own product or service, or another they know. If you, the teacher, also do this exercise, it will be beneficial at the third stage.

Exercise 2

Students work in pairs to write a marketing email to customers about a new product or service. Students may need ten minutes for this task.

Exercise 3

Students swap emails with another pair and underline the motivating words. They then give each other feedback. Encourage them to suggest improvements, or any other words which could be used to motivate the customer.

> **EXTRA ACTIVITY**
> You could ask students to find examples online, or take photos of adverts in magazines or on the streets which use these words, and bring them to class next time.

Progress test

Download and photocopy *Unit 2 Progress test* and *Speaking test* from the teacher resources in the *Online practice*.

Unit content

By the end of this unit, students will be able to
- talk about projects
- run update meetings and question decisions
- talk about past or recent actions and achievements.

Context

It is often said that management is based on four stages: assess, plan, do and evaluate. This is certainly true of managing projects. Many projects fail or come up against problems because most emphasis is placed on the 'doing' stage – carrying out the tasks required to complete a project. However, experienced project managers know that equal importance should also be given to the stages before and after in order to ensure project success.

Assessing what is required, followed by a period of planning, will let a manager know how many people, what expertise and how much money will be needed. Afterwards, the manager needs to evaluate how effective the work has been before possibly proceeding to the next part of the project.

Not all of your students will necessarily be managers and they won't always be in charge of major projects, but much of their work will include completing minor projects or being involved in the process. They will also be used to working in teams and collaborating on projects, perhaps with companies in other countries.

The first part of this unit looks at the various stages involved in working on a project, some of the problems which can occur, and presents vocabulary for discussing the progress of projects. Students move on to develop their skills in meetings and focus on the language for giving an update on progress. *Language at work* focuses on the key grammar used for talking about the recent past and giving updates. The *Talking point* allows students to practise the language of the unit within the context of finding solutions to common problems when working on projects.

Starting point

Encourage students to tell the class about any projects they are currently involved in.

PRE-WORK LEARNERS Students could describe a project in their home life, such as redecorating the house or planning an event, or one they're involved in at school or college.

Working with words

Exercise 1

As a lead-in to the exercise, ask students if they have ever been to a theme park, and what they know about the kinds of 'rides' that can be found. Find out about any particularly good or bad experiences they've had.

Students work in groups and use the picture to elicit six stages in such a project.

Exercise 2

Students join with another group, share their stages and add any new ideas to their list. You could put some of their ideas on the board.

Exercise 3

Students then read the article and compare their ideas with those mentioned. Afterwards, discuss the stages and see how they compare with everyone's suggestions in **2**.

Check students understand *to storyboard* – to produce a series of drawings or pictures that show the idea or a plan of how something will work (the term originally comes from the world of film, and planning stories and plots). Also check *to outsource* – to arrange for somebody outside a company to do work or provide goods for that company.

Possible answers
brainstorming, storyboard the ideas, present ideas to project manager with suggestions for time and budget, project gets go-ahead, engineers and other designers are involved, safety testing and assessment, launch date, visitor feedback

Exercise 4

Students work in pairs. They read the questions and then read the text again to find the answers.

Answers
1 to survive in this competitive world, and because each year visitor expectations are higher
2 not too controlled ('no idea is considered too crazy at this stage as there are no budget constraints')
3 the concept, a forecast of the time needed to complete the project and a realistic budget
4 in order not to miss the deadline, and because the project will need a wide range of people with specialist skills
5 a team falls behind schedule or goes over budget
6 by the number of visitors choosing to go on the ride; by monitoring visitor feedback and surveying visitors

Exercise 5

Students match words 1–10 with a–j to make phrases from the article. They can check their answers by finding the phrases in the text in **3**.

Answers

1 e 2 a 3 b 4 d 5 h 6 g 7 c 8 i 9 j 10 f

PRONUNCIATION Ask students to underline the word stress in these words from the text: *realistic, budget, schedule, accurate, forecast, planning, constraints, deadline*

Answers

rea<u>lis</u>tic, <u>bud</u>get, <u>sche</u>dule, <u>a</u>ccurate, <u>fore</u>cast, <u>plan</u>ning, con<u>straints</u>, <u>dead</u>line

Exercise 6

Students can work in pairs to decide if they associate the phrases in **5** with being successful, unsuccessful or both.

Answers

Successful (S): upfront planning, accurate forecast, realistic budget, stay on track, make the launch date
Unsuccessful (U): miss the deadline, run into problems, go over budget, fall behind schedule
Both: budget constraints

Exercise 7

Students choose a phrase from **5** with a similar meaning to the words in bold to complete the sentences. Remind students to make sure their choice makes sense within the context of the rest of the sentence. They can check their answers with a partner.

Answers

2 realistic budget
3 budget constraints
4 make the launch date
5 accurate forecast
6 fell behind schedule

PRONUNCIATION Point out that *schedule* can be pronounced in two ways: both /ˈskedʒuːl/ and /ˈʃedʒuːl/ are possible. Ask students to look again at the phrases in **7** and to check which word in each phrase is stressed.

Answers

1 upfront <u>planning</u>
2 <u>realistic</u> budget
3 <u>budget</u> constraints
4 make the <u>launch</u> date
5 accurate <u>forecast</u>
6 fell behind <u>schedule</u>

Exercise 8

Students choose the verb which goes with all three phrases in each group. They can do this in pairs.

Answers

1 run 2 miss 3 stay 4 go 5 make

DICTIONARY SKILLS
A good dictionary will supply more information about these verbs, and many of the phrases and collocations in **5** and **8** will appear. Students could be encouraged to use the dictionary to find and check their answers.

Further practice

If students need more practice, go to *Practice file 3* on page 110 of the *Student's Book*.

Exercise 9

Students work in pairs. They read the notes about the project review. They could put a tick or cross against the different parts to indicate what has gone right and wrong. Encourage them to use phrases from **5** and **8** in their discussion. You could put these phrases on slips of paper, give a set to each pair, and ask them to turn each one over as they use them.

ALTERNATIVE Students could decide in advance which phrases they want to try to use; they could also tick off the phrases in the book as they use them.

Exercise 10

Students work with another pair and compare lists. You could also make this competitive between pairs and see who can use the widest range of expressions for describing the project.

Listen and make notes on any difficulties the students have with any of the phrases from **5** and **8**, and then conclude this section with feedback on pronunciation and use of the words and phrases.

EXTENSION Ask students to compare the successes and failures of this project with their own projects, in or outside work. You could also ask them to come up with a list of suggestions for managing a project successfully.

Photocopiable worksheet

Download and photocopy *Unit 3 Working with words* worksheet from the teacher resources in the *Online practice*.

Business communication

Exercise 1

▶ **3.1** As a lead-in, ask students to work in pairs. They have two minutes to list all the features they have on their phones, e.g. texting, games, Internet, etc. See which pair has the longest list. Next, give them another two minutes to think of new features they would like manufacturers to add to their phones. Collect their ideas for a 'super phone' on the board. Students read the *Context* about the Tech-Tariff project to understand the background for the listening. Also allow time for them to study the agenda for the meeting. Expect to play the listening twice.

Suggested answers
2 has a realistic schedule and extra time has been planned
3 booked two weeks ago
4 already received offers, most within budget, final choice not made yet
5 problem with handset battery life – can run out in six hours
6 may have to reschedule

Exercise 2

▶ **3.1** After students have listened and answered questions 1–3, they can compare their answers with the *Key expressions*. Note that a number of the phrases include the present perfect tense, which is dealt with later in this unit.

Refer students to the *Tip* about the word *things* at this stage, since it appears in three of these phrases.

Answers
1 How are things with …? / How's the … coming along? / How far are you with …? / How does your side of things look?
2 So what do you mean exactly? / So what you're saying is …? / So the real problem lies with …?
3 Up to now … / We've set … / We're on track. / He booked the venue two weeks ago. / I've already … / I haven't made a final choice yet. / Things aren't running as smoothly as I'd hoped. / We've hit a problem with …

Exercise 3

▶ **3.2** Explain to students that they are going to hear the later part of the meeting. Students listen and answer the questions.

You may have to explain the phrase in the answer to question 2. *Their reputation is at stake* means that not saying anything about the poor battery life may affect the good opinion that customers have of the company or brand.

Answers
1 It wouldn't help meet the deadlines.
2 Their reputation is at stake.
3 They will look at what they can reschedule.

Exercise 4

▶ **3.2** Students listen for the phrases to complete the suggestions. You will probably need to play the listening again for students to note the responses. Note that these responses are negative or show reluctance.

Answers
a How about finding
   Response: I don't think that would help us …
b We could
   Response: That's possible, but …
c Why don't we wait
   Response: That's not an ideal solution.
d would be my proposal
   Response: I'm not convinced.
e If you ask me, we should
   Response: I suppose so.

Further practice

If students need more practice, go to *Practice file 3* on page 110 of the *Student's Book*.

Exercise 5

Students will need some time to study their 'To do' lists and notes before making their call. They are going to ask each other for an update on each item on the list, as well as making and responding to suggestions. Encourage them to use as many of the phrases for asking for / giving an update as possible.

Afterwards, ask each pair to report back on what action is still required.

Make notes as students role-play the situation and give feedback on correct use of the phrases.

EXTRA ACTIVITY
Ask students to write their own current 'To do' list, including one or two items that are already (partially) completed. Working with a partner, in turn they should ask each other questions about each item on the list, and find out which items on the list have been completed. For anything not done, they should ask more questions to find out why, and when it's expected to be finished. Encourage them to think about time and cost, and other people involved in these tasks. Students should explain to each other any problems they have run into which have caused delays, but avoid trying to blame others.

Photocopiable worksheet

Download and photocopy *Unit 3 Business communication* worksheet from the teacher resources in the *Online practice*.

Practically speaking

Exercise 1

Students read the questions and discuss their ideas with a partner. Try to encourage them to discuss real examples. Elicit one or two comments from the group.

Exercise 2

▶ **3.3** Before playing the listening, ask students to look at the three topics and to predict what words or phrases they might hear. Students then listen to three conversations and match each to a topic.

Answers
a 3 **b** 1 **c** 2

Exercise 3

▶ **3.3** Students listen again and tick the expressions they hear.

Check students understand the use of *given that* in *given that we're buying* when you consider something; here, you could replace *given that* with *as* or *considering*.

Answers
1 (in conversation 1), 4 (in conversation 2), 5 (in conversation 3)

Exercise 4

Students work in pairs and each makes a list of three decisions. They then tell each other about them and their partner asks questions or comments to make sure they made the right decision.

Remind students that as these are decisions that have already been made, they should be sensitive to criticizing each other: listening carefully and responding in a genuine way, as well as using their voice appropriately (intonation and sentence stress) will help.

Refer students at this point to the *Tip*, for sounding less critical.

When they have finished, find out whether individuals feel they did in fact make the right decision(s), or whether they are now not sure!

Give feedback on use of the phrases in **3**.

EXTRA ACTIVITY

Ask students to imagine a new situation at work or in their place of study, e.g. the introduction of a new kitchen/coffee system, providing drinking water or using social media. Students should work in groups of four or five, or as a whole class group. In turn, one student puts forward a decision; the next person responds by questioning the decision, using one of the phrases from **3**. The next student should respond and either support student 1 or adapt the decision. Example:

S1 As the summer's coming, we're going to provide drinking water and plastic cups on each floor of the office.

S2 Are you sure that's the best way forward?

S3 Well, it's important that everyone drinks enough water to be able to work well.

S4 Sorry, but I'm not sure I agree. And I think it's a waste of plastic.

S5 We could provide water, but we all use our own cup, etc.

Allow three to five responses, before starting with a new situation.

Language at work

Exercise 1

Students work in pairs to decide which tense is used.

Answers
present perfect: a, b, d, e   past simple: c, f

Exercise 2

Students answer the questions in the *Language point* by reading the sentences again in **1**.

Answers
1 b, d   **2** c, f   **3** a, e   **4** already   **5** yet

Grammar reference

If students need more information, go to *Grammar reference* on page 111 of the *Student's Book*.

Exercise 3

When deciding which time expressions can be used with each tense, students will find it easier to make complete sentences with the expressions to test their ideas. Also, refer them back to sentences a–f in **1** to note the time expressions used. Students could work in pairs to do this activity so that they can discuss the differences in meaning.

Answers
1 last week, a couple of weeks ago, yesterday
2 up to now, so far (this week), since our last meeting, to date, just, over the last few months
3 The expressions *today* and *this morning* could work with either. The past simple will refer to a finished action: *We spoke this morning*. We could also use the present perfect if the action has occurred this morning or today and it is still recent: *We've worked on it this morning* (and it is still the morning or very recent).
In the last month could also be used with either. If you are talking on the 30th of the month, you might say *In the last month we've sold 12,000 units*. However, if the month is in the past, we would use the past tense: *2004 was an excellent year, and in the last month we sold 20,000 units*.

Further practice

If students need more practice, go to *Practice file 3* on page 111 of the *Student's Book*.

Exercise 4

Students work in pairs. They read their information in the back of the *Student's Book* and take turns to ask and answer questions about their progress on the project. Before they start their discussions, check they are clear about the progress on their project and what has/hasn't been done.

Check understanding of the following: *to convert* – to change or make something change from one form, purpose, system, etc. to another; *plumbing* /ˈplʌmɪŋ/ – the system of pipes, etc. that supply water to a building.

Listen in and give feedback on students' use of the two tenses immediately after this role-play, as they will need to use the present perfect or past simple again in the next activity.

Exercise 5

Students now work with a different situation. They read about the context at the back of the *Student's Book* and then decide which items on the 'To do' lists have or haven't been done.

When they are ready, they take turns to ask and answer each other about each one.

> **EXTRA ACTIVITY**
> To provide some consolidation of the grammar point and some writing practice, ask students to write an email to their colleague giving an update on what has been done on the 'To do' list.

Exercise 6

Students work with a partner. They each think of five goals or plans they've had recently. These could relate to study, work or personal plans. You could suggest they write them down and include one or two details about when they achieved each goal, or if not, why not.

> **EXTRA ACTIVITY**
> Ask students to think about their language learning and where they were six/12/24 months ago: Did they have any clear aims and reasons for learning English, and how have they progressed so far? Are there any things they haven't yet achieved? Why might this be? You could encourage them to make short- and long-term plans about what they will be able to use their English for, e.g. next week, in a month, in three months, etc.

> **Photocopiable worksheet**
> Download and photocopy *Unit 3 Language at work* worksheet from the teacher resources in the *Online practice*.

Talking point

Discussion

Exercise 1

Ask students to look at the infographic about five common problems and see if they agree. They can discuss this in pairs and add any other problems to the list.

Exercise 2

Students discuss which of the problems they have experienced and what happened in each case. You could elicit some ideas and find out how similar their experiences were.

PRE-WORK LEARNERS Ask students to consider these questions in relation to another project they have been involved in (regardless of whether money was involved), e.g. family projects, moving house, redecorating part of their flat/house, planning a holiday or event, a school or college team project.

Exercise 3

Students discuss what they have learnt and what they now do differently. Elicit from each student one learning point they would like to share with the others.

PRE-WORK LEARNERS Students should consider mistakes made on previous projects they have been involved with (see above, after **2**, for ideas), and discuss what they learnt and what they would do differently as a result.

Task

Exercise 1

Students work in groups to prepare a presentation. Working from the list of problems, they should come up with the five best solutions. You could suggest students make a list of problems and then brainstorm together solutions to prevent the problems.

Students could then choose the best solution for each problem. Make sure each student is clear about the best solution.

ONE-TO-ONE Students use the project problem list to prepare a list of solutions. You could either work together, or each prepare a separate list of solutions and then compare them.

Exercise 2

Regroup students so that there is one person from each group in each of the new groups. In turn, each student presents their previous group's list of solutions. The others should listen and compare the solutions with their own.

When they have finished, find out how similar the groups' suggestions were.

EXTENSION Ask students, in their groups, to decide on the best solution they heard to each of the five problems and to share them with the class.

> **Progress test**
> Download and photocopy Unit 3 *Progress test* and *Speaking test* from the teacher resources in the *Online practice*.

Viewpoint 1

Preview

The topic of this *Viewpoint* is *Learning in business*. Students begin by watching a short introductory video about the Saïd Business School, and compare it to any formal training of their own.

Students then watch an interview, in two parts, with Peter Tufano, the Dean of the Saïd Business School, who describes the types of students who attend and how the school differs from other business schools.

In the final part, students consider different ways of learning and apply these methods to some of their own familiar contexts, deciding which would be appropriate and discussing why.

Exercise 1

Students read the questions and then share their answers with a partner. Open up the discussion with the whole class.

PRE-WORK LEARNERS Students can discuss any recent or current training they are doing. They might also be interested to consider how closely this relates to any work they have in mind, or planned, for the future. Also ask if they plan to do any further training, and whether this is likely to be formal or informal.

Exercise 2

▶ 01 Students read the bullet point list. Check they understand what is meant by *executive education* (education for those already working in higher business positions) and *custom programmes* (programmes which are made specifically for participants' needs). Play the video and ask students to take notes. If necessary, pause after each section to allow writing time. You may need to play the video twice. Students can compare answers in pairs.

ALTERNATIVE With a weaker group, you could elicit or give a possible example for each category first, before playing the video, e.g. Location and age: Manchester, 200 years old; Facilities: lecture hall, 15 classrooms, etc.

Answers

Location and age: Oxford. The school was founded in 1996 (but the university is 800 years old).
Facilities: a 300-seat auditorium; a library with over 11 million printed titles as well as access to digital resources; an outdoor amphitheatre for lectures, theatre performances and musicals.
Undergraduate and MBA programmes: undergraduate programme in economics and management, and several postgraduate programmes, such as in law and finance, and the Oxford MBA programmes.
Executive education and custom programmes: for more experienced students who would like specially designed courses (intensively over a few days or for longer study) that can be combined with online learning.
World ranking: one of the top-ranked business schools in the world.

Exercise 3

▶ 02 Students should read the profile of Peter Tufano first. They then read the topics a–e and watch the first part of the interview with Peter Tufano to order the topics. You may need to play the video more than once, pausing after each section.

Answers
a 3 **b** 4 **c** 2 **d** 1 **e** 5

EXTRA ACTIVITY

Ask students to draw up a table of features of the Saïd Business School mentioned in the first and second parts of the video. This will include those listed under **2** and **3**. Then ask students to note down answers and information according to where they studied or are studying. If students are studying at the same college, they could do this in pairs. Encourage them to include any other aspect not listed which they consider significant.

When they have finished, ask them to discuss with a partner which different features about their own place of study they think are the most relevant, important and/or interesting, and are good selling points for the institution.

Exercise 4

▶ 02 Students read the seven questions and then watch the video again to find the answers.

Answers
1 modern and forward-looking
2 strategy and accounting, about marketing, about operations and the fundamental building blocks of business
3 artificial intelligence, attitudes towards globalization, what's happening in the workplace, demographic change that's changing customer bases
4 somewhere between 18 and 21 years old; they're smart, they're motivated, they're ambitious young people
5 has five years of experience, late 20s and they come from all over the world
6 They might have 10, 15 years or more of experience – experience in the public sector, in the private sector, managing and running just about everything and anything.
7 Anything is possible when you sit down next to a Saïd Business School student.

Exercise 5

Students read the questions and discuss them in pairs.

PRE-WORK LEARNERS Ask students not yet in work to think about additional study courses they could take part in to support their current interests and course of study. Alternatively, they could think of a totally different career path they have in mind – perhaps a dream job! – and discuss together how they would learn the necessary skills and what course(s) they could take.

ALTERNATIVE Students may have stories about people they know who have gone back to college, or started new studies later in life and then completely changed careers. Encourage them to share their stories and – if they know – compare any different experiences of studying (online vs face-to-face, different aged students, different nationalities).

Exercise 6

Students read the words and phrases on the left and match them to the definitions. Do one together first.

Answers
1 h 2 d 3 g 4 a 5 f 6 c 7 e 8 b
Check students' pronunciation of the following:
synchronous /ˈsɪŋkrənəs/; *asynchronous* /eɪˈsɪŋkrənəs/;
pedagogy /ˈpedəɡɒdʒi/; *tutorial* /tjuːˈtɔːriəl/.

Exercise 7

▶ 03 Students read the questions and then watch the video to listen for the answers.

Answers
1 synchronous vs asynchronous, reading vs listening, building and creating vs analysing
2 Because people learn differently.
3 It's an effective way to analyse a (real) situation, and allows you to imagine yourself in the middle of that situation and make decisions as if you were a business leader.
4 It allows slowed-down thinking.
5 Because some things are best learnt through direct experience, such as learning how to work with a team, how to deal with failure and how to stay focused on customers.
6 All methods work and sometimes it's great to be able to stretch yourself by testing different kinds of learning methods.

EXTENSION Referring back to some of the vocabulary in **6**, you could ask students for any brief examples of their own when they have experienced asynchronous as opposed to synchronous learning, or studied using a case method approach.

Exercise 8

Students first read the list of different ways of learning. They will then decide whether it is suitable for the three options, i.e. learning a language, learning a new work skill, or for a hobby.
You could start by brainstorming work skills (e.g. using a new team-working website, storing documents in a corporate filing system, etc.), and other hobbies (e.g. oil painting, golf or another sport, cooking, photography).
Do the first one together and elicit students' ideas. Then let students work alone to work through the list.

Exercise 9

Ask students to work in small groups. For each way of learning, encourage students to clarify and explain their answers and listen to others who may have different experiences.

You could demonstrate the first one with the whole class.

Allow students to change their answers if they are persuaded by others' experiences!

When students have worked through the list, encourage them to share other ways of learning which they have experienced and how effective they were.

Finally, ask groups to work on a brief summary of their feelings on the most effective ways of learning; you could ask for a spokesperson to report this information to the rest of the class.

You could open up these ideas for whole-class discussion, especially as this may affect students' approach to language learning during this course.

ONE-TO-ONE You can both work through the list individually in the same way and then discuss and compare your answers, as well as discuss any other effective ways of learning.

EXTRA ACTIVITY
Ask students to choose two ideas from the list of ways of learning which they are less familiar with, but would like to try. Give them time to decide how they could try them out, and what they would be learning, e.g. vocabulary; understanding fast English or different accents; learning something new at work; working on their own hobby. Challenge them to try these for a week and report back next time. Students can then share their ideas and experiences and compare notes. Encourage them to evaluate how effective the method was and how they might adapt or use it in future.

Further ideas and video scripts
You can find a list of suggested ideas for how to use video in the class in the teacher resources in the *Online practice*. The video scripts are available to download from the Teaching resources on the Oxford Teachers' Club. www.oup.com/elt/teacher/businessresult

4 New ideas

Unit content

By the end of this unit, students will be able to
- talk about innovation
- present ideas and refer to evidence
- talk about ability in the past, present and future.

Context

Not all your students will necessarily think of themselves as innovators. Many people link the topic 'new ideas and innovation' to those who 'invent'. But while inventions require innovation, all businesses will flourish with staff who are innovative in their thinking.

New ideas and innovation have taken on even greater importance in recent years with the growth in fields such as software development, design and marketing. Companies such as Microsoft or Apple have become global giants through their attention to innovation. Steve Jobs, the charismatic co-founder and CEO of Apple until 2011, explained that his company's success with products such as the iconic iPod music player has come about by 'saying no to 1,000 things' ('The Seed of Apple's Innovation', *Business Week*, 12 October 2004). In other words, innovation requires many ideas before arriving at the best, so companies with a culture of welcoming any new idea, however crazy, are more likely to succeed than those that don't have this culture.

The first part of this unit presents language for talking about ideas and innovation before moving on to the language for putting forward new ideas, products and services in the context of a formal presentation. This is supported by a language section on talking about ability, which will allow students to describe and discuss changes in technology, systems and ways of working. The *Talking point* extends the idea of innovation and creativity through a brainstorming activity.

Starting point

Discuss the first question together to establish the difference between *invention* and *innovation*. It might be better to allow students to think about and discuss questions 2 and 3 in pairs before comparing their answers with the rest of the class.

Answer
1 *Invention* usually refers to a machine or new system. *Innovation* refers to both inventions and new ideas or concepts.

PRE-WORK LEARNERS Ask students to consider an innovation that would help them study better, or something to improve the quality of their life at college; they could consider physical ideas, or even an app!

Working with words

Exercise 1

Students read and discuss the questions with a partner. Elicit some ideas from the class, and encourage students to give examples and reasons.

PRE-WORK LEARNERS For the first question, ask students to think about any special awards that exist in their college: they could also consider the aim of the award, how motivating it is, and how winners benefit.

Exercise 2

Students will find the answers to questions 1–2 in the text. You can point out that sustainable energy tends to use energy produced by clean technologies, e.g. solar power. Draw students' attention to the way in which the Ashden Awards encourage people to be innovative.
Check students understand *sustainable* – it has two meanings: 1. involving the use of natural products and energy in a way that does not harm the environment, e.g. *sustainable forest management*, and 2. that can continue or be continued for a long time, e.g. *sustainable economic growth*. Both are relevant here.

Answers
1 The charity rewards and promotes sustainable energy solutions in the UK and developing countries. It aims to raise international awareness of the benefits of sustainable energy in order to deal with climate change and improve the quality of people's lives. It also aims to encourage more people around the world to find new ways of meeting energy needs and to change the thinking and policy among governments and non-governmental organizations (NGOs).
2 It gives cash prizes, publicizes the winners in order to encourage others to follow their example, and brings together the winners and main decision-makers of governments and organizations.

Exercise 3

▶ **4.1** Students read the questions and listen for the answers.

Answers
1 Bridges to Prosperity provides bridges over rivers in developing countries. It is sustainable because it facilitates travelling by foot (rather than car) and also uses locally-sourced materials, avoiding the need to use expensive equipment with a large carbon footprint. Greenlight Planet provides affordable and safe solar-powered lighting to developing countries. It is sustainable because it uses solar power to generate electricity.
2 The bridges mean people can buy and sell locally-produced goods, children can go to school, and doctors and nurses can travel to every part of the region.
   The solar-powered lights get round the problem of no electricity, at an affordable price through monthly instalments.

Exercise 4

Students work in pairs to match the adjectives in A to the nouns in B.

Answers
poten̲tial be̲nefit
prac̲tical so̲lution
cutting-e̲dge techno̲logy
i̲nnovative ap̲proach
comme̲rcially-v̲iable propo̲sition
ma̲jor bre̲akthrough
key co̲ncept
Other combinations:
key be̲nefit; poten̲tial so̲lution/bre̲akthrough; i̲nnovative solution/techno̲logy; ma̲jor be̲nefit; comme̲rcially-v̲iable solution.

PRONUNCIATION Check students can say the collocations in **4**. Drill them and make sure students are stressing the correct syllable (see underlined syllables in Answers above).

Exercise 5

Students work in pairs to create their sentences.

ALTERNATIVE Suggest that students create sentences, but leave gaps for the adjective–noun combinations. They then exchange their gapped sentences with another pair, who try to guess the missing combination.

Exercise 6

Students can work in pairs to match the phrasal verbs to 1–9.

Answers

1 get round	4 take forward	7 bring down
2 bring about	5 pay off	8 take up
3 come up with	6 carry out	9 set up

PRONUNCIATION Remind students that stress is on the particle (not the verb) in phrasal verbs, i.e. get ro̲und; bring abo̲ut.

Exercise 7

The two texts are about projects which won Ashden Awards. Students complete them with the correct phrasal verbs from **6**.

Answers

1 come up with	4 taken up	7 carrying out
2 get round	5 bring about	8 paid off
3 set up	6 take forward	9 bring down

DICTIONARY SKILLS
At this level, make sure students are aware of the difference between transitive and intransitive verbs, and how dictionaries can help. Point out that transitive verbs are followed by an object, e.g. *come up with an idea*. Intransitive verbs don't necessarily need an object, e.g. *the work has paid off*. So in **6**, *paid off* is the only intransitive verb; the rest are transitive. Ask students to look up these two examples in a good dictionary. The symbols [T] or [I] are shown next to the verb.

Further practice

If students need more practice, go to *Practice file 4* on page 112 of the *Student's Book*.

Exercise 8

Allow time for students to brainstorm ideas before preparing their talks. The talks could be given to the class or two groups can meet to present their innovations. You could give them the following ideas to get them started:
• training and study via distance learning
• changes to transport to help save energy
Remind them also to refer back to the models in **7** if they need help structuring their ideas.

Photocopiable worksheet

Download and photocopy *Unit 4 Working with words* worksheet from the teacher resources in the *Online practice*.

Business communication

Exercise 1

Students read the questions. Discuss them as a class. Encourage students to give reasons for their opinions.

PRE-WORK LEARNERS Ask students to think about the security issues at their school or college. This could also include personnel.

Exercise 2

▶ **4.2** Allow time for students to read the *Context* and look at the slides before listening. They will probably need to hear the listening twice to make their notes and check them.

Answers
1 Overview of the product
2 Advantages for your company
3 Demo video
4 state-of-the-art security
5 iris recognition
6 are identified by unique patterns in their iris
7 scans their iris
8 compares with a central database

Exercise 3

▶ **4.2** Students listen again and complete the sentences with key phrases for giving a talk.

> **Answers**
> 1 three things
> 2 give you a brief overview of
> 3 'd like to show you
> 4 sound OK
> 5 is a state-of-the-art security system
> 6 How does it work

Exercise 4

▶ **4.3** Students read the questions and then listen to the second part of the presentation to answer them.

> **Answers**
> enhanced security / no one can copy your iris
> increased flexibility / control which employees have access

Exercise 5

▶ **4.3** Students listen for the key phrases. You'll probably need to play the listening at least twice. Afterwards, students can compare their phrases with the language in the *Key expressions*.

> **Answers**
> a There are two main benefits of … / the biggest potential benefit is … / This means that … / The other major advantage is … / And here is another great thing
> b in comparison to your current … / whereas you can't … / However, with …
> c Now I'd like to move on to …

Further practice

If students need more practice, go to *Practice file 4* on page 112 of the *Student's Book*.

Exercise 6

Students work in pairs and take turns to present the slides in **2** using the *Key expressions*.

Refer students to the *Tip* and phrases for linking ideas. They could practise the language by writing four sentences to contrast ideas about their own product, workplace or place of study. For example: *Although you may have heard the company has had losses recently, we are now back in profit.*

PRONUNCIATION Point out that we often use our voice to help an audience understand, by stressing key words and pausing between phrases. Ask students to look at their answers in **5**, to underline words they would stress, and indicate with a forward slash [/] where they would pause, e.g.
There are two main benefits … The other major advantage is … However, / with the DiScan2 iris …
Students could practise this by reading aloud an extract from the audio script on page 143 of the *Student's Book*, and then relate these ideas to their own talks.

Exercise 7

In this exercise, students practise the phrases using an idea of their own. If students need help with suggestions, here are some possible ideas to present:
- a new smartphone app
- the company or college website, or a new web page
- security around the (company or school) building

During the presentations, make notes on correct and incorrect use of phrases. You could ask students to comment on one thing they liked about their colleagues' presentations and one thing they would do differently.

ALTERNATIVE Students could use their idea from **8** in *Working with words*. This time, they present the same content but in a more formal presentation style. The benefit of this is that students are familiar with the content so can concentrate on using the new phrases.

Photocopiable worksheet

Download and photocopy *Unit 4 Business communication* worksheet from the teacher resources in the *Online practice*.

Practically speaking

Exercise 1

Students read the questions and examples of evidence. Encourage them to tick any they have used and to share any specific examples they can remember.

> **Possible answers**
> academic studies – to support reasons for changing something
> market research – to argue for a new type of product or service
> interviews and questionnaires – to show customer results and reactions
> examples of existing users – to show potential users what other people have said / used the product for
> medical evidence – to explain why people's eating or exercise habits should change
> personal experience – to tell an anecdote or story to get your audience emotionally involved

PRE-WORK LEARNERS Students will probably be familiar with giving presentations as part of their studies, or remember mini-presentations they gave at school.

Exercise 2

▶ **4.4** Students will hear two questions from the audience, with answers. If necessary, recap on the key information in the listening in **2** and **4** from *Business communication*. They should listen for the different types of evidence referred to.

> **Answers**
> academic studies, medical evidence and examples of existing users

Exercise 3

▶ **4.4** Students listen again and complete the sentences with the verb they hear.

> **Answers**
> 1 show 2 suggests 3 demonstrates

EXTENSION Ask students what other verbs could be used to refer to evidence, e.g. *highlight, clarify, illustrate*, etc.

Exercise 4

Students work alone in this exercise. Encourage them to come up with at least two different types of evidence which could explain the benefits of their chosen product or service.

Exercise 5

Students now work with a partner and listen to each other's sentences. Ask listeners to explain why the evidence makes the product or service sound more convincing.

When giving feedback, focus on evidence for the product or service, and how it makes it sound more convincing.

Language at work

Exercise 1

▶ 4.5 Students read the questions, and then listen for the answers. They can compare their answers with a partner.

You might need to pre-teach the following before listening: *marina* = a place where leisure boats are kept; *pilot project* = a stage of product development when you test it for the first time; *patent* = a legal document to allow inventors to sell the idea/product; *exclusive contract* = a contract allowing one person/company to sell a product.

Answers
1 It's a specialist Internet service provider that provides wireless Internet access at all the major marinas in the country.
2 They can only access it on land or they have to have the right technology.
3 They'll be able to access the Internet from their boats for a basic monthly fee.
4 They have exclusive contracts in all the major marinas in the country for the next seven years.

Exercise 2

Students read the ten extracts and match each one to whether it refers to the present, past or future (a–c). Note that although some extracts refer to inability (3, 9,10), they can still be categorized as present, past or future.

Answers
a 3,6   b 1, 5, 8, 9   c 2, 4, 7, 10

Exercise 3

To complete the rules, students will find it useful to look at the words/phrases within the context of the extracts in **2**.

Answers
1 can, is/are able to
2 be able to
3 has/have been able to
4 could
5 was/were able to, couldn't, wasn't/weren't able to

EXTENSION To give practice, and help students differentiate between verbs when talking about ability in the past, ask them to match the four sentence halves below.

1 *I bought some Bluetooth headphones, but …*
2 *John downloaded a new app and …*
3 *We tried to set up a new Wi-fi system and finally …*
4 *When I was a teenager, …*

a *… he was able to send free messages to anyone within 500 metres.*
b *… I couldn't make them work with my tablet.*
c *… I could run 5 km in 25 minutes!*
d *… we managed to connect all the computers!*

Answers
1 b   2 a   3 d   4 c

Then ask the following questions about the second part:
Did it happen once? Is it positive or negative?
If positive, was it difficult?
Remind students that we can use *was(n't)/were(n't) able to* in <u>all</u> situations; *managed to* is used when the situation is difficult. Now ask students to write a sentence using each of the verbs about themselves.

Grammar reference
If students need more information, go to *Grammar reference* on page 113 of the *Student's Book*.

EXTRA ACTIVITY
Before starting **4**, tell students to close their books. Ask them to make notes about the past, present and future as you read about the new technology: read the example text about mobile phones in **4**. Afterwards, students can open their books to check their notes. This is a helpful lead-in to **4**.

Exercise 4

Students can work in pairs and take turns to talk about the technologies or work together to prepare mini-talks.

Further practice
If students need more practice, go to *Practice file 4* on page 113 of the *Student's Book*.

Exercise 5

Students work in pairs and discuss technological changes which affect their lives.

Before students have the discussion, it will be helpful for them to think about the past, present and future in the category they choose. For example, for 'vehicles' they could plan their thoughts like this.

Past	Present	Future
• no combustion engine • couldn't travel very far • slow speeds • not much storage space	• travel long distances comfortably • good storage space • radio and CD player	• use biofuels or run on solar power • be 100% non-polluting • will be able to fly

While they are discussing, listen in and focus on use of tenses and the verbs they use for talking about ability. Then afterwards, give feedback on how the students talked about ability in the past, present and future. Don't forget to highlight good uses of how they described ability, too!

EXTENSION Students could, in pairs, choose one idea, and present it to the rest of the class, highlighting past facts with future hypotheses. Other students could then vote on which pair has the best ideas for the future.

Photocopiable worksheet
Download and photocopy *Unit 4 Language at work* worksheet from the teacher resources in the *Online practice*.

Talking point

Discussion

Exercise 1

Ask students to look at the title of the text and to remember a recent conversation when they used 'Yes, but…', or 'Yes, and…'. Were they agreeing or disagreeing with the other person? What was the effect of their comment? Then ask students to read the text and compare their ideas.

Elicit their ideas. You could also try to get students to give examples of when they say 'Yes, but…', or 'Yes, and…', in English, or their own language.

PRE-WORK LEARNERS For this exercise, and **2** and **3**, suggest students consider their own role as students, the behaviour of teaching staff, or others they know who are in business.

Exercise 2

Students read the questions and share their ideas with a partner. You could then brainstorm two lists to write on the board: one with success factors and one with fail factors.

Exercise 3

Students read the question and share their ideas with a partner. Elicit a few ideas from the class.

Task

Exercise 1

Students work in groups to think of innovative features for bicycles for children. You could give them a time limit, e.g. five minutes. Remind them that they should write down all the ideas that are mentioned.

In order to engage students in the best way possible, you could suggest that they try to draw or sketch their ideas; these could form the basis of clarification, if necessary.

ONE-TO-ONE Work together to brainstorm a list. You could start by brainstorming individually for two minutes, then brainstorming together for a further three minutes, telling each other your ideas first and then adding any more which come to mind.
You could write down each joint idea yourself. Then read out the list and together choose the best five ideas.

Exercise 2

One student reads out the list and together each group decides on the best ideas.

Exercise 3

Ask a different student from each group to present the group's ideas to the class. The other groups should listen and compare this with their own list. Encourage students to explain or validate their choice, and listeners to ask any questions for clarification.

EXTENSION Ask students how effective they found the 'Yes, and…' approach: how did it help them add ideas and be positive?

Exercise 4

Students could work in the same, or different, groups. They should come up with an item related to their business.

PRE-WORK LEARNERS Ask students to choose an idea related to their college, e.g. course material, classroom layout, course evaluation, etc.

Progress test
Download and photocopy *Unit 4 Progress test* and *Speaking test* from the teacher resources in the *Online practice*.

Unit content

By the end of this unit, students will be able to
- talk about ethical business
- plan arrangements and respond to invitations
- talk about decisions, plans and predictions.

Context

Consumers are increasingly affected in their choices by how they perceive the ethical behaviour of companies. More and more of us are asking questions about well-known brand names such as: Where are the products made? How much are the staff paid? What are their working conditions like? What is the source of the raw materials and are they environmentally friendly? Is there a huge financial imbalance between the company's profits and its struggling supplier in the developing world? Being ethical has become a PR issue with consumers, governments and pressure groups all watching businesses carefully for signs of ethical or unethical practices.

In response, many companies have policies on corporate social responsibility (CSR). The central idea of CSR is that corporations should make decisions based not only on financial factors but also on the social and environmental impact of their activities. Company websites generally outline CSR activities, e.g. health and safety policies, projects with the local community and environmental initiatives. The impact on the employee is that they could be asked to become involved in charity work or raise money for a good cause, or concern for the environment may lead to changes in working practices. During the course of this unit, you might want to find out from students if their employers' ethical approach has had an effect on their working lives.

This unit presents vocabulary to enable discussion of ethical issues. The context in *Business communication* follows a company wishing to promote its ethical ethos and allows students to practise language for explaining future plans and making invitations/recommendations. In the *Talking point*, students discuss corporate standards, then consider a list of personal standards to help take care of their own ethical position regarding work.

Starting point

Students discuss the three questions. Ask them to give examples of real companies they have heard about, where possible.

Possible answers

1 Some of the areas may include: paying fair prices for goods (e.g. to workers in developing countries), pollution from factories, using recycled materials, giving staff incentives to share cars to work, sponsoring local charities/events.
2 Many countries have companies which are known for social responsibility. For example, The Body Shop has always promoted itself and its products on the basis of its ethical principles.
3 In recent years, various clothing companies like Gap and Nike were accused of exploiting cheap labour in poor working conditions to produce garments for high-street stores. For some time, they suffered some image problems and have worked hard to counter this by stressing their ethical principles.

EXTRA ACTIVITY

Ask students to visit the websites of a few companies they are familiar with and to look for information about the company's ethics. For example, most oil companies will offer information on work they are doing to help the environment. Similarly, companies such as The Body Shop have clear ethical positions. This mini-research project will work especially well with pre-work learners.

Ask them to report back in the next lesson on what they discovered.

Working with words

Exercise 1

Students brainstorm the characteristics of an 'ethical business'. Afterwards, write everyone's ideas on the board in preparation for the reading in **2**.

Possible answers

concerned about its impact on the environment
pays a fair salary to employees
charges a fair price
is ethical in its financial dealings (e.g. with shareholders)
gives a proportion of its turnover or time to non-profit activities
which are beneficial to the local community

Exercise 2

Students read the questions and then read the text. While reading, students check if any of the ideas on the board from **1** are referred to.

Exercise 3

Students first read the questions and then read the text again. Questions 1–4 can be answered by reading the text. Question 5 can be discussed as a class.

Answers

1 They are people who love 'wild and beautiful places' and therefore 'take an active part in the fight to repair the damage that is being done to the health of our planet'.
2 It is committed to protecting the environment. It shows this by donating time, services and at least 1% of sales to environmental groups.
3 They work to reduce pollution, and use recycled polyester and organic cotton.
4 They have stayed true to their principles over the last thirty-plus years.

> **EXTRA ACTIVITY**
> To introduce the theme of the next activity, which includes a focus on rules and regulations controlling ethical behaviour, ask students if they know of any rules in their country governing issues such as pollution and the environment. Is their company or field of business affected by these rules?

Exercise 4

Students match words from each column to make phrases. They then use the phrases to complete the questions.

Answers

1 comply with regulations
2 donate time
3 reduce the impact
4 act responsibly
5 take an active part in
6 stay true to its principles
7 share a strong commitment to

Exercise 5

Students work in pairs, asking and answering the seven questions from **4**. If there is time, ask them to report back on what they learnt to the class.

Exercise 6

▶ **5.1** Students first read the questions and then listen to the interview. They do not necessarily listen for single words to answer these questions; they will need to interpret the tone of the speakers and make notes on what is said.

Answers

1 The interviewer's style is quite aggressive.
2 The spokesperson's response is calm and he replies to each question with examples of the good work his company is doing.
3 a It has a reputation for fairness, and combats discrimination and prejudice within the organization; it improves working conditions and safety; it has schemes for staff education, health and training.
  b It has reduced its methane and hydrocarbon emissions and provides financial support for turtle conservation in Bangladesh.
  c It has set up a community project to provide skills training for unemployed youths in Sangu, and health initiatives and other schemes to encourage sustainable livelihoods in Rajasthan.

Exercise 7

Students can refer to audio script 5.1 on page 143 of the *Student's Book* to read some of the words in context and decide whether they are ethical or unethical.

Answers

1 ethics, responsibility, fairness, generosity, values, credibility
2 bribery, deception, corruption, prejudice, greed, discrimination

Exercise 8

Students work in pairs to come up with a situation to explain the meaning of each noun. Read the first one together.

> **EXTRA ACTIVITY**
> Give each student one of the words on a piece of paper. They stand and find a partner and, in turn, try to elicit the word from their partner by describing or giving a definition or example of the word. When they have both guessed each other's words, they swap, find a new partner, and repeat the process.

Exercise 9

Students can work in pairs to complete the table. Suggest they use dictionaries to check their answers.

Answers

deception – deceptive
responsibility – responsible
fairness – fair
generosity – generous
credibility – credible
ethics – ethical
corruption – corrupt
prejudice – prejudiced
greed – greedy
discrimination – discriminatory

PRONUNCIATION Check students know where the word stress is in each of the words in **9** (see the underlined syllables in Answers above).

Exercise 10

Students read about companies X and Y on page 136 of the *Student's Book*. X clearly has a positive ethical policy whereas Y requires negative words to describe it.

Check students understand the following words used in the profile about Company Y: *to corrode*; (*oil*) *leak*; (*oil*) *spill*; (*oil*) *refinery*; *petroleum coke* (a by-product of the oil refining process; also known as 'petcoke').

Listen, and give feedback on students' use of the vocabulary in **7** and **9**. Focus on collocations and phrases, and word stress.

Further practice
If students need more practice, go to *Practice file 5* on page 114 of the *Student's Book*.

Photocopiable worksheet
Download and photocopy *Unit 5 Working with words* worksheet from the teacher resources in the *Online practice*.

Business communication

Exercise 1

Students read the questions and discuss their answers with a partner. You could elicit or give an example first, e.g. check and confirm the availability of any staff who will be involved in the visit. Elicit ideas from the group.

Exercise 2

▶ **5.2** Students begin by reading the *Context*. You can check their understanding by writing these questions on the board (answers are shown in brackets).

1 *What is Hummingbird Teas?* (a company which sells speciality teas)
2 *What is its USP?* (its ethos)
3 *Where does it buy its tea?* (from small local farmers)
4 *Why does it need Clare?* (to raise its profile)
5 *Who has been invited to see the operation?* (reporters/journalists)

Students listen and make any changes to the notes.

> **Answers**
> Trip to China (not South Africa) is confirmed
> Four days at one tea plantation
> No opportunities for sightseeing
> Two dates: February (15th–20th; need bookings by January 10th) and one in May
> A lot of road travel and one internal flight

Exercise 3

▶ **5.2** Students listen again and complete the phrases.

> **Answers**
> 1 'll email you the final itinerary
> 2 we're planning to show you
> 3 idea is to
> 4 'll get the opportunity to
> 5 we're going to arrange

Exercise 4

▶ **5.3** Students read the questions and then listen to the second part of the meeting to answer them.

> **Answers**
> 1 Watch the tea being prepared and sample local specialities produced by the cooperative, visit a project to help build a school, visit the site of a reforestation scheme, talk to the coordinators of the business in China.
> 2 Stay with the guide who can interpret (because no one speaks English).

Exercise 5

▶ **5.3** Students listen again and complete the phrases. Refer students to the *Tip* when dealing with the answer for 2.

> **Answers**
> 1 'd like to invite you to
> 2 we strongly recommend you stay
> 3 you're also welcome to visit
> 4 sounds, 'd like to take you up on that
> 5 would be a good idea to
> 6 is highly recommended
> 7 well worth a visit
> 8 That's not really what
> 9 we'd be delighted to
> 10 it's just the kind of thing I need

EXTENSION Suggest students write down two recommendations for someone visiting their company or college: one using *advise* and one using *recommend*.

Exercise 6

Students can work in pairs to categorize the phrases and then check their answers in the *Key expressions*.

> **Answers**
> **a** 1, 3, 9   **b** 2, 5, 6, 7   **c** 4, 8, 10

PRONUNCIATION With many of these phrases, a speaker will emphasize certain key words to sound more genuine and polite. Write these phrases from the *Key expressions* on the board and read them out, stressing the underlined words.

You're <u>welcome</u> to … We'd be <u>delighted</u> to …
We <u>strongly</u> recommend you … It's <u>highly</u> recommended.
It's <u>well</u> worth a <u>visit</u>.
That would be <u>great</u>.
That sounds <u>really</u> interesting.
It's <u>just</u> the kind of thing I need.
That's not <u>really</u> what I'm <u>looking</u> for.

Alternatively, students can say which word they think is stressed. Then play the listening again for students to listen to which words are stressed.

Further practice

> If students need more practice, go to *Practice file 5* on page 114 of the *Student's Book*.

Exercise 7

Students work in A/B pairs and use the information to make invitations and recommendations, using the *Key expressions*. Encourage them to sound interested by stressing the right words and using lively intonation to show enthusiasm, e.g.

A *We'd like to invite you to an information day about Hummingbird Teas and fair trade.*
B *That sounds <u>great</u>! I'd <u>like</u> to take you <u>up</u> on <u>that</u>.*

Exercise 8

Allow about five minutes for students to prepare their ideas in 1 before working with another partner in 2. If your students are all from different companies, they could do the first task alone. Students who don't work for a company can use the company in the information on page 136 of the *Student's Book*.

PRE-WORK LEARNERS Students can complete **8** using the company in the information on page 136 of the *Student's Book*. However, they could also imagine their school or college is having an open day for students who are thinking of enrolling next year. They then follow the same procedure as in **8**.

Photocopiable worksheet
Download and photocopy *Unit 5 Business communication* worksheet from the teacher resources in the *Online practice*.

Practically speaking

Exercise 1
Students can read and discuss the questions in pairs. Elicit some of their ideas or experiences.

Exercise 2
▶ **5.4** Students listen and decide how the person responds in each case.

Answers
1 c **2** b **3** a **4** d **5** e

Exercise 3
▶ **5.4** Students listen again, and write down any useful phrases they hear. Encourage them to show their lists to a partner, before suggesting the phrases below.

Possible answers
How about joining us …?
That would be nice, but can I let you know later?
Do you feel like …?
Sorry – I'm heading …
Would you like to go to …?
Why not? Sounds good.
I was wondering if you'd like to come with me.
That's very nice of you, but I'm fairly sure I've got something on – I'll have to check …
Are you interested in coming along?
Thanks for the invitation, but I'm not sure I can. I'm waiting to see if I have to …

Where appropriate, draw attention to the following.

- *How about …?* and *Do you feel like …?* are followed by a verb in the *-ing* form.
- *Why not?* is a strange way to accept but basically means 'I can't think of a reason why not'. In translation this may sound rude, but in English it is perfectly acceptable.
- We often follow *Sorry* with the present continuous form of the verb to explain why the invitation is being declined.

EXTENSION Ask students if they know of any other ways of responding to invitations: accepting, declining, hesitating, e.g. *I'd love to!* is strong acceptance, while *Well, actually, …* could be used to introduce an apology and explanation for not accepting.

Exercise 4
For this activity, ask students to stand and walk around the classroom to make their invitations.

As you listen, focus on the use of accurate phrases for inviting and responding to invitations and give feedback accordingly.

ONE-TO-ONE In this activity, as the teacher, you could play different roles for the student, e.g. a colleague, their boss, a family friend, etc. In each case, state who you are. Then ask the student to do the same for you.

Language at work

Exercise 1
At upper-intermediate level, this activity should offer a review of future forms. However, if any of the grammar is new for students, follow up with the exercises in the Practice file on page 115 of the *Student's Book*.

Students read the sentences and label the tenses.

Answers
a present continuous	**d** present simple
b *will* + infinitive	**e** *will* + infinitive
c *to be going to*	

Exercise 2
Students match sentences a–e from **1** to situations 1–5 in the *Language point*.

Answers
1 e **2** c **3** a **4** b **5** d

Grammar reference
If students need more information, go to *Grammar reference* on page 115 of the *Student's Book*.

Exercise 3
Ask students to work in pairs and choose the best option in each sentence. During the feedback stage, ask them to explain why it is better.

Answers
1 I'm doing (The speaker has already got an appointment on Friday. It isn't an instant decision.)
2 it'll be (The forecast is a prediction of tomorrow's weather.)
3 arrives (The event is timetabled.)
4 I'll let (The speaker makes an instant decision after hearing the new information.)
5 I'm going to go (The speaker has already made a plan for Monday. It isn't an instant decision.)
6 I'm meeting (The speaker has already got an appointment for this afternoon.)
7 I'll email (The speaker makes an instant decision in answer to the question.)
8 will notice (Greta isn't at work yet. The speaker is making a prediction.)

Exercise 4

Although the questions are straightforward for this level, students might not respond with the appropriate future form so you will have to monitor carefully. Note that responses to 1, 3 and 8 are likely to use *going to*; 2, 6 and 7 could use present continuous; 4 expects the present simple; *will* is likely to be used in 5 but feasibly will crop up in any of the answers. Note, however, that many students try to overuse *will* to avoid the other future forms. This is something that can be commented on in feedback afterwards.

Further practice
If students need more practice, go to *Practice file 5* on page 115 of the *Student's Book*.

Exercise 5

Students write and explain their important dates.

Give positive feedback when students are able to use a range of future forms to explain their dates. If students only use one or two forms, ask them to repeat the activity and try to use a wider and more meaningful use of forms; they could do this in new pairs. Weaker students may benefit from writing their ideas down first.

PRE-WORK LEARNERS Students could write down dates relating to their own studies, their career plans or key dates in their college calendar.

Photocopiable worksheet
Download and photocopy *Unit 5 Language at work* worksheet from the teacher resources in the *Online practice*.

Talking point

Discussion

Exercise 1

Students can discuss these questions in pairs and compare ideas with the class. Students then read the article and compare their ideas.

Exercise 2

Encourage students to try to work out the meaning of each phrase from context, and elicit examples they are familiar with.

> **Possible answers**
> In this situation, *to stink* means to seem very bad, unpleasant or dishonest; for example, if a business is corrupt or giving out false information; *to cross the line* here implies there is an imaginary line beyond which you should not go; if you do, you are doing something bad or perhaps illegal, e.g. taking an idea from another company and using it as your own.

Exercise 3

Allow students to discuss their ideas for this question in pairs; if they all work for the same company, it might need to be dealt with sensitively, e.g. by saying that students do not need to talk about their own company. If appropriate, elicit some of their ideas.

PRE-WORK LEARNERS You could give students one or two situations where they could discuss what they would do, e.g. a car manufacturer which saves money by not putting safety features as a top priority; a pharmaceutical company which bribes doctors to prescribe their medicines; a technology company (e.g. smartphone manufacturer) which forces its workers to do long overtime hours regularly.

Exercise 4

Students read the questions. They could compare ideas with a partner, before you open up the discussion to the class.

> **EXTRA ACTIVITY**
> Ask students to find out about their own company's or college's commitment to society and report back next time.

Task

Exercise 1

Students work individually, look again at the five personal standards, and decide which ones they would include in their list. Ask them also to consider any other standards they would introduce.

Exercise 2

Students work in groups of three or four and compare their answers. Remind them to give reasons.

ONE-TO-ONE Brainstorm a list individually, based on the list of personal standards in the article. Then, for **3**, compare lists and put together a list of seven standards.

Exercise 3

Students work in groups to write a longer list of personal standards they all agree with.

Exercise 4

Students present their list to the other groups.

To encourage them to listen to each other, you could ask them to listen and find out if any other group has similar ideas to their own. Alternatively, you could ask them to discuss, agree as a group and vote on which other group they think has the best list.

Progress test
Download and photocopy *Unit 5 Progress test* and *Speaking test* from the teacher resources in the *Online practice*.

Unit content

By the end of this unit, students will be able to

- talk about personality
- participate in decision-making meetings and talk about social plans
- talk about different quantities.

Context

It is said that the most successful business people are quick to make decisions and slow to change them. On the other hand, Napoleon Hill in his classic guide to motivation and success, *Think and Grow Rich* (1937), said that 98% of us end up in our jobs because we are indecisive.

To achieve, businesses must be able to make decisions. This doesn't only mean decisions at a board or strategic level, as decision-making is a skill which all employees need. Of course, we all make decisions in different ways. The widely used Myers-Briggs Type Indicator separates us into Thinkers and Feelers. Thinkers approach their final decision by studying the facts and taking time. Feelers base their decision on intuition and their senses. The Myers-Briggs Type Indicator also offers other categories which are presented in *Working with words*. The Indicator is a type of personality test which allows managers to analyse their teams and categorize the decision-making approaches of their staff. For example, someone who is a Thinker may find the approach of a Feeler frustrating. However, at the same time, by combining different types of decision-makers, a manager is able to create a well-balanced team or assess where weaknesses in the decision-making process may occur.

As well as looking at the vocabulary of personality in this unit, students practise the language for giving and responding to arguments and opinions in decision-making meetings. *Language at work* reviews and extends students' knowledge of countable and uncountable nouns, and expressions of quantity. In the *Talking point*, students discuss differences between how different people, according to gender and age, make decisions. Students then design a questionnaire to find out more about decision-making processes and use the questionnaire to interview other students.

Starting point

Students can briefly discuss the two questions. Responses will highlight students who are Thinkers (those who are guided by facts and need more time) or Feelers (those who follow intuition and work under pressure) in their decision-making.

Working with words

Exercise 1

Students read the question and discuss their opinions with a partner. Elicit some of their ideas, with specific examples or experience.

Exercise 2

Before students read the text, ask them to look at the eight personality types in the question headings (extrovert, introvert, etc.) and guess which type matches to 1–4. They can then read the text and check their guesses.

Answers

1 judger   **2** thinker   **3** extrovert   **4** intuitive

EXTENSION   Ask students to decide which one of each pair they think they might be. Keep this very brief at this stage.

Exercise 3

Students match the adjectives to the statements, then compare answers in pairs.

Answers

2 methodical	**7** outgoing	**12** tactful
3 indecisive	**8** thoughtful	**13** self-contained
4 determined	**9** creative	**14** focused
5 instinctive	**10** conventional	**15** impulsive
6 flexible	**11** rational	**16** pragmatic

PRONUNCIATION   Ask students to find the words with three or four syllables in 1–16 in **3** and to categorize them according to where the stress falls. Then drill the words as necessary.

Answers

three syllables: de<u>ter</u>mined, in<u>stinc</u>tive, <u>flex</u>ible, <u>ra</u>tional, out<u>go</u>ing, cre<u>a</u>tive, self-con<u>tained</u>, im<u>pul</u>sive, prag<u>ma</u>tic

four syllables: me<u>tho</u>dical, inde<u>ci</u>sive, con<u>ven</u>tional

Exercise 4

Students work in pairs and use the adjectives in **3** to describe the type of people they like / don't like to work with. Correct any word stress or pronunciation problems on the spot.

Exercise 5

For question 1, students can underline the parts of the text which answer a and b. For question 2, refer students to the *Tip* for an explanation of *good at* and *good with*.

Answers

1 Extroverts – good with people / prefer to do lots of things at once

Introverts – prefer to focus on one thing at a time and be behind the scenes

Sensors – good at understanding details and remembering facts and specifics

Intuitives – like to focus on the big picture and future possibilities / prefer to learn new skills

Thinkers – prefer to remain detached

Feelers – good at complimenting

Judgers – like to complete projects

Perceivers – like to be flexible and keep options open / like to start projects / prefer to play now and work later

Exercise 6

Students now decide which personality type they are most like in each section in the text and write down the first letter for each type (e.g. ESTP). The key on page 139 of the *Student's Book* is a long summary of the different combinations, so advise students to read just their own analysis. If they are interested, they can read the rest of the key after the lesson. Ask students to report back on how accurate they think their analysis is.

Exercise 7

▶ **6.1** Students listen and decide which of the personality types applies to each speaker. This is quite challenging, as they have to listen and will probably need to refer back to the text to compare the personality types with what they hear. Students could compare their answers in pairs, or check in the audio script on page 144 of the *Student's Book*. For further discussion, ask students to say which speaker they think gives the best advice.

Answers

Speaker 1: I   **Speaker 2:** N   **Speaker 3:** T   **Speaker 4:** J

EXTRA ACTIVITY

As a follow-up to the listening and to reuse the vocabulary in this section, ask students to choose one of the personality types and write a short paragraph like the speakers in the listening. They can write about themselves or make up a fictional speaker describing their type. When they have finished, they read out their description to a partner or the class and the listeners have to guess which personality type they are describing.

Exercise 8

If students have difficulty matching or want to check their answers, play the listening again.

Answers

weigh up information	have confidence in (my) own
delay my decision	judgement
rely on feelings	get different perspectives
trust my instincts	decide between two things
consider all the options	

EXTRA ACTIVITY

Other combinations are possible with the words and phrases in **8**, so you could ask students to create some. Encourage them to make full sentences so the new combinations appear in context. For example: *You need to weigh up all the options when making a decision so you can choose the best thing to do.*

Possible answers

weigh up all the options / two things

delay judgement

get information

trust judgement / feelings / information

consider feelings / information / instincts

have confidence in my instincts/feelings

rely on information/instincts

Exercise 9

Students use the phrases in **8** to tell their partner about a recent decision they made. Allow students a minute or so to make notes about the decision. You can also ask them to note the following details:

- How did you arrive at the decision?
- What were the options?
- What affected your final decision?
- Looking back, was it the right decision?

Remind students that it doesn't have to be a decision at work. It might be about how they chose a course at university, or a decision about shopping at the weekend.

Further practice

If students need more practice, go to *Practice file 6* on page 116 of the *Student's Book*.

Exercise 10

Students work in pairs. They refer back to the information in the text to decide on the personality types for each job. Encourage them to use the vocabulary from **2**, **4** and **7**. For example, they might decide that introverts, intuitives, feelers and judgers would make good website designers because a designer needs to be creative and focused, would need to rely on their instincts and would need to be good at thinking of new design ideas, etc.

Make notes on students' responses and give feedback after the task. Listen out for correct combinations of verb–noun phrases and drill any problematic pronunciation.

Photocopiable worksheet

Download and photocopy *Unit 6 Working with words* worksheet from the teacher resources in the *Online practice*.

Business communication

Exercise 1

Students read the questions and can share their ideas with a partner. Perhaps elicit or give an idea first, for each question, e.g. some people speak too much or for too long; the leader of a meeting needs to involve everyone present.

Exercise 2

▶ 6.2 Students read the *Context*. Check they understand the basic meaning of *budget deficit* – more money has been spent than was planned. Ask how many people are at the meeting (four in total = three regional managers and one consultant).

Students listen and tick the points discussed.

> **Answers**
> Points 2, 3 and 5 are discussed.

> **EXTRA ACTIVITY**
> Ask students to look at the list of points and discuss if any of these are ever discussed where they work. Has their company implemented any of the points to help reduce spending?

Exercise 3

▶ 6.2 Students listen again and complete the phrases. For 2, point out that *here in black and white* is a commonly used idiom referring to black writing on white paper. It means that the speaker has the facts, or proof.

> **Answers**
> 1 if we look at the facts, we'll see that
> 2 Look at, here in black and white
> 3 thing is
> 4 A classic example is
> 5 what you're getting at
> 6 not convinced
> 7 I'm concerned
> 8 is right, I think it would be crazy to

Refer students to the *Tip* for more on the idiomatic phrase in sentence 5.

Exercise 4

Students refer to Sinead's part in audio script 6.2 on page 145 of the *Student's Book* and focus on the language for leading a meeting. You could do the first one together.

> **Answers**
> 1 Today, I'd like to establish …
> 2 Jens, could you start us off, please? / Hang on, let's hear what Jens has to say about …
> 3 What's your position on this?
> 4 Can we move on to …? / Let's turn to the next item …
> 5 I don't want to spend too long on this point.
> 6 Let's draw up some action points on what we've discussed so far.

Further practice

If students need more practice, go to *Practice file 6* on page 116 of the *Student's Book*.

Exercise 5

1 First, ask students to study the agenda item and to add two of their own ideas. Let them share their ideas with a partner.

2 This stage is included to encourage students to use new phrases rather than relying on simpler ones they already know. Draw students' attention to the *Key expressions* and tell them to focus on the top four categories. Note that no one is specifically leading the discussion so students don't need to choose from that list. (If you want them to focus on these phrases as well, you will need to rotate the person leading during the meeting every 3–5 minutes.) You may need to take in small pieces of card or paper.

3, 4 Divide the class into small groups. They should role-play and continue the meeting from **2**, using the phrases they chose. Encourage other students to listen carefully and check the phrases are used correctly. You may have to be the final judge in such cases. At this stage, don't give too much feedback. The aim here is for students to become familiar with new phrases before using them in a free practice situation in **6**.

> **ONE-TO-ONE** You could ask your student to think of one or two other people they know well, who might have very different opinions to them. Allocate phrases from the *Key expressions* to each of you, including the 'other person or people'. Then, as you run the discussion, ask your student to 'play' phrases from the other people, too.

Exercise 6

Students follow the stages for the budget meeting. Give time for students to work through each stage. If you think students will need help with ideas for stage 1 (e.g. pre-work learners), you can suggest the following.

Your department is Sales. The five suggestions are:

1 increased expense allowances for travel

2 laptops for everyone in the department

3 company cars

4 bonuses and cash incentives for increased sales

5 a Christmas party.

Also make sure that students take turns to lead the discussion and use the phrases from **4**.

Give feedback on the use of the phrases and how effectively different students lead the discussion.

> **ONE-TO-ONE** You could follow the same procedure for a discussion as with the idea for **5**, or ask your student to represent two different people with different views. You could also do the same. You should then each make two lists with three suggestions each, with each list representing a different person. Then add reasons to support your opinions. You should then be able to run the meeting.

> **EXTENSION** As an extra idea, you could ask students to audio record their meeting (e.g. using a smartphone), and then play it back: while they listen, they should note down (or tick off) the phrases they hear, and afterwards comment on how effectively they feel the meeting went, and why.

Photocopiable worksheet

Download and photocopy *Unit 6 Business communication* worksheet from the teacher resources in the *Online practice*.

Practically speaking

Exercise 1
Students read the question and write down three small talk questions. Then elicit a few ideas and find out how similar their ideas were.

Exercise 2
▶ **6.3** Students listen and establish how certain each speaker is about plans. You will probably have to explain the phrase in conversation 2: *We'll probably catch a movie*. In this context *catch* means 'see' a movie.

> **Answers**
> **a** 4 **b** 1 **c** 5 **d** 2 **e** 3

Exercise 3
▶ **6.3** Students listen again and note down the phrases for each category.

> **Answers**
> 1 What've you got on …? / What are you up to …? / Are you taking any time off …? / What are you doing …? / Anything nice planned for …?
> 2 Well, I'm supposed to be … / We'll probably … / It depends on … / We're off to … / Nothing special.
> 3 Poor you. / Sounds good. / I see. / Lucky you!

Exercise 4
It will help if students are standing so they can move around the room and ask different people about their plans. You could join in, and help students move round and talk to several people.

> **ONE-TO-ONE** Each of you could take on two or three roles, e.g. a colleague at work, a good friend, a friend you know less well, and you could ask and answer these questions in different roles.

Language at work

Before starting this section, check that students understand the terminology in **1** and **2**. Some students may have previously seen the terminology *count* and *non-count nouns* rather than the terms *countable* and *uncountable nouns*.

Exercise 1
Students do the matching task.

> **Answers**
> **a** problem, point **b** expenses, savings **c** waste, overtime

> **DICTIONARY SKILLS**
> It will be very useful for students to use a dictionary with the next activity. Make sure they know how to identify countable and uncountable nouns in a dictionary with the symbols [C] and [U].

Exercise 2
Students can work in pairs to do this activity.

> **Answers**
> **C:** product, colleague, suggestion, fact, journey, proposal, document
> **U:** news, information, travel, accommodation (note that in American English you can have *accommodations* as a plural noun), software, correspondence, money, equipment, insurance, advice
> **B:** expenditure (= general spending and can also refer to different areas of spending), paper (= paper in general, and 'a paper' given in an academic situation, 'a paper' referring to 'a newspaper'), business (= the whole area of business and individual businesses), experience (= people's experience and different experiences in our lives), time (= time in general and 'remembering times in our lives', for example)

Exercise 3
To help students group the quantifiers, they could experiment with them in their own sentences. They can also check their answers by reading the information in the *Grammar reference*.

> **Answers**
>
> | Expression of quantity | + noun |
> | --- | --- |
> | a, an, the, one | *product*
colleague, expenditure, paper, suggestion, business, experience, time, fact, journey, proposal, document |
> | too many, not many, a few, fewer, very few | *facts*
products, colleagues, expenditures, papers, suggestions, businesses, experiences, times, journeys, proposals, documents |
> | lots of, plenty of, more, most, some, not enough, hardly any, not any, no | *news*
expenditure, paper, information, business, travel, experience, time, accommodation, software, correspondence, equipment, insurance, advice |
> | too much, not much, a little, less, very little | |

Grammar reference
If students need more information, go to *Grammar reference* on page 117 of the *Student's Book*.

Exercise 4

Students complete the sentences.

Answers			
1	very little	5	any
2	fewer	6	enough
3	too much	7	too many
4	some	8	a

Draw students' attention to the *Tip* and suggest they write down two sentences for themselves to illustrate the difference.

Further practice
If students need more practice, go to *Practice file 6* on page 117 of the *Student's Book*.

Exercise 5

Before speaking, students will find it helpful to make lists of differences between each of the situations listed. Give students an example of a comparison if they need help, e.g. *The really nice thing about working for a small family firm is that I have lots of contact with the owners. We understand each other well and there are very few communication problems. On the downside, there's very little opportunity for promotion and, when we're together, there's hardly any difference between 'work and play'. That can be tricky.*

Exercise 6

Again, students should start by making lists of what they need more or less of. If they need ideas, they can comment on things like public transport, traffic, entertainment, shopping, accommodation or restaurants, Internet access at work, office space, etc.

EXTENSION You could encourage students to give peer feedback by listening out for correct use of quantifiers during the activities in **5** and **6**.

PRE-WORK LEARNERS Students can consider how to improve their place of study, e.g. its facilities.

Photocopiable worksheet
Download and photocopy *Unit 6 Language at work* worksheet from the teacher resources in the *Online practice*.

Talking point

Discussion

Exercise 1
Students first answer the question, and then read the text to compare their answers.

Exercise 2
Ask students to share their opinions on the information in the text with a partner or in small groups. Elicit one or two ideas, asking them to give reasons.

Exercise 3
You could suggest students think more critically about the information and consider where the information came from.

Task

Exercise 1
Groups decide on five or six situations where people have to make decisions at work.

PRE-WORK LEARNERS Students could consider one of the following decision-making situations: what topics to include in a course; how to schedule classes; how to recruit more students, etc.

Exercise 2
Students then design a questionnaire. Questions could relate to issues such as time, gender, age, on- or offline work, etc.

Exercise 3
Students interview people from other groups.

ALTERNATIVE Students could interview colleagues and friends outside class and then bring their results back next time.

ONE-TO-ONE You could suggest your student interviews colleagues at work, or friends. Alternatively they could make a list of ten people and decide how they think each one would answer the questions.

Exercise 4
Students compare the information with their original group. They should then create a chart and present it to the class. They should also come up with any obvious conclusions: for this part, suggest they refer back to the bullet point information in the text. Ask listeners to ask questions, as well as suggest their own conclusions.

Progress test
Download and photocopy *Unit 6 Progress test* and *Speaking test* from the teacher resources in the *Online practice*.

Preview

The topic of this *Viewpoint* is *Consumer behaviour*. Students begin by reflecting on something they have bought recently and the factors which influenced their purchase. They then watch three parts of an interview with a leading expert in consumer behaviour; these focus on customer mood, the location of price in advertising and gender issues. Finally, they work together in groups to consider how to improve the customer experience for a given business, based on the research on mood, price and gender.

Exercise 1

Students first think about a product they have bought recently. They then read the bullet point list of factors and decide how important each factor was, on a scale of 1–5, in influencing their decision to buy the item.

Exercise 2

Students consider any other factors which influence their decision-making, e.g. what others are saying about the product, fashion, how necessary it is, etc.

Exercise 3

Ask students to work in small groups. They should tell each other about the product they bought and which factors affected their decision-making. Encourage them to provide as much information as possible, and also to ask each other questions for clarification or more information. Elicit any particularly interesting points to the whole class.

Exercise 4

Ask students to read the words and phrases 1–12 on the left, and match them to the definitions a–l. You could do one together first.

Answers
1 f 2 e 3 d 4 h 5 c 6 g 7 a 8 b 9 i 10 k
11 l 12 j

PRONUNCIATION Some of these words are difficult to pronounce. You could divide the class into three or four groups and ask each group to look up three words (i.e. group 1 looks up words 1–3, and so on). Ask students to look the words up (in a paper-based dictionary if you have them, or in a good online dictionary), and to 'become the experts' for the pronunciation of their three words. They should be able to pronounce each word accurately, which means focusing on individual sounds, as well as word stress. Remind them to check the definitions in the dictionary with the meanings listed in **4**.

Then regroup the students so that each person is working with new partners: they should teach each other how to pronounce their words, focusing on both sounds and word stress. Listen in and help out if necessary.

Exercise 5

▶ 01 Students read the topics A–C and then watch the first part of an interview with Nancy Puccinelli about customer behaviour. They should put the topics in order.

Answers
1 B 2 A 3 C

Exercise 6

▶ 01 Students read the five questions and then watch the video again to answer them.

Answers
1 an undercurrent of how we feel
2 because we're tired or suffering from lack of sleep
3 strong(er) visceral emotions / emotional states
4 giving too much information and taking up too much time / not reading the situation / customer's emotions
5 by quickly selecting an appropriate bottle of wine that looks acceptable at a reasonable price

Exercise 7

Students read the questions. They could discuss their answers and experience first with a partner, then you could open the discussion up to the whole class if they are happy to share their stories.

Exercise 8

Ask students to look at the advert, and ask them to decide which place on the advert would be best for putting the price. Share their answer with the whole class. (You could do this by illustrating it on the board so that everyone can see, and so that all their suggestions are visible, too.)

Exercise 9

▶ 02 Students now watch the second part of the interview and compare what they hear with their prediction in **8**. You may need to play the video twice.

Answer
on the right-hand side

Exercise 10

▶ 02 Students read the five statements and try to remember if they are true or false. Then play the video again. You could also pause the video after each short section and ask students to share with a partner the key information from that section.

Answers
1 T 2 F 3 T 4 T 5 F

EXTENSION Ask students if they are surprised by the outcome, and if they heard anything specific or interesting. Ask for their own experiences of pricing and where it is placed. You could also ask students to be extra aware of this issue outside class and to report back on anything interesting they find for the next class.

If students have questions about some of the other words and phrases the speaker uses, draw their attention to the *Glossary*.

Exercise 11

Ask students to work in small groups. They should read the questions and discuss their experiences together. Share anything particularly interesting with the whole class.

Exercise 12

▶ 03 Before you play the video, ask students to read the five statements. Then play the video. Students underline in each case whether it is 'men' or 'women' for the conclusions on the research.

ALTERNATIVE Ask students to guess which gender is the answer for each sentence before they watch the video. They can then compare their predictions as they watch the video.

Answers
1 women
2 women
3 men
4 men
5 women

EXTENSION Ask students if they are surprised by the results and/or if they agree with them, according to their own personal experience.

Exercise 13

Ask students to work in small groups. They should read the three questions and then discuss them together. Ask students to share with the group any specific ideas, especially from question 3.

PRE-WORK LEARNERS Ask students to answer these questions in relation to a company or product they know well, or their area of study.

Exercise 14

Ask students to work in groups again. It's probably a good idea to suggest this time they work with different partners.

In this section, students will be putting into practice the three issues discussed in the video: mood, price and gender.

First, as a group, they should decide on what sort of retail business they want to focus on, e.g. a series of small supermarkets, a chain of cafés or restaurants, etc. They should then work through each of the three items on the agenda and decide what action they will take to improve the customer experience in each case.

ONE-TO-ONE You could decide on the type of retail business together, and then work on and discuss the first item on the agenda together, too. You could then each look at one of the other two items before sharing your ideas for these together.

Exercise 15

Students regroup so that they are working with different partners. In turn, they should go through the items on the agenda and tell each other how they will improve the customer experience.

EXTENSION Ask each group to decide on one or two best ideas for improving the customer experience and to share these with the class.

Further ideas and video scripts

You can find a list of suggested ideas for how to use video in the class in the teacher resources in the *Online practice*. The video scripts are available to download from the Teaching resources on the Oxford Teachers' Club. www.oup.com/elt/teacher/businessresult

7 Outsourcing

Context

Outsourcing emerged during the 1980s as businesses looked at ways to reduce costs and compete in the global economy. Companies assessed which parts of their operations were 'non-core' and gave these to other companies to run and manage. This allowed a company to focus on its 'core competencies'. It also let the company make better use of the emerging opportunities made available by access to a worldwide labour force. This access was fuelled by the development and boom in telecommunications networks. Consequently, many manufacturing industries are able to move operations overseas, which is referred to as 'offshoring'.

While in the 'noughties' (2000s), the BRICS economies (Brazil, Russia, India, China and South Africa) were important emerging economies, ten or fifteen years on, the countries most likely to do well are Mexico and Colombia in Latin America, Kenya in sub-Saharan Africa, Malaysia, Indonesia and India in Asia, and just one country in Europe – Poland. Aside from these expectations, the fastest growing countries of the world are now Ethiopia, Uzbekistan, Nepal and India.

By definition, then, outsourcing and offshoring have resulted in much more communication between people from different countries with different languages and cultural backgrounds. Many of your students may be working for businesses which either outsource or are involved in providing services to another business. In the first section of the unit, they will have the chance to comment on and discuss the pros and cons of outsourcing. In *Business communication*, students practise the language for presenting factual information objectively within the context of an outsourcing situation. In the *Talking point*, students consider and discuss tasks and jobs which can, or could, in the future be done by robots.

Starting point

Make sure students understand the concept of 'outsourcing' (see *Context* for further information). It's quite possible that many students will already be familiar with the term and use it in their own language.

Discuss each question as a class. For question 3, you could ask students to come up with a list and elicit their ideas to the board.

PRE-WORK LEARNERS Students may be able to answer the questions. However, they could also answer them by referring to large companies in their country.

Possible answers

3 Almost any part of a company's work can be outsourced, apart from its core skills. One of the most typically outsourced business tasks is customer support, where call centres in, for example, India will take this over at a much lower cost. Similarly, accounting and tax preparation are often outsourced, but only if these practices are appropriate to the country. Web design, computer programming and engineering require specialized skills, and are often outsourced if templates or routine tasks are involved. For cost and employment issues (social health care, etc.), manufacturing is also often outsourced. And of course, research and development, which includes market surveys, are typically outsourced, as long as the firm being outsourced to understands the type of research needed for the project in question.

Working with words

Exercise 1

Students read the title and try to guess what the article could be about. Prompt them with question words, e.g. *Where? When? How? Why?* Share some of their ideas with the group.

Exercise 2

Students read the article quickly to compare their predictions in **1**.

Exercise 3

Students read the questions and then read the article again. They can share their answers with a partner.

Answers

1 Outsourcing in India tends to be for services rather than manufacturing as in China.
2 Western businesses were attracted to India in the early part of the twenty-first century because they could outsource routine work and concentrate on core activities.
3 The profits from outsourcing allowed India to invest in infrastructure and training facilities.
4 Three reasons why outsourcing might slow down: (1) Salaries have risen so there aren't the same cost savings. (2) There isn't anything left to outsource. (3) Companies are relocating previously outsourced parts of their business closer to home so they can have better control.

PRONUNCIATION Provide some practice with the vowel sounds /ɔː/ and /əʊ/. Write the following on the board: *core, growth, outsource, offshore, locations, export*. Ask students to categorize the words into two groups according to the vowel sound (note that it is the underlined sound in *outsource, offshore* and *export*). Then ask them to add three more words to each category.

Answers and possible extra words
/ɔː/: *core, outsource, offshore, export, sport, four, law*
/əʊ/: *growth, locations, phone, loan, cope*

Exercise 4

Students match the words in bold from the text to the definitions.

Answers

1 sector	7 skilled workers
2 infrastructure	8 business process outsourcing
3 core activities	9 outside expertise
4 outsourcing vendors	10 offshore locations
5 training facilities	11 cost-saving
6 export growth	12 closer to home

EXTENSION Ask students to choose one or two of the words or phrases and say how it is relevant in their own company, or a company they know, e.g. (about a language school) *Our core activities include language teaching in the city, but we also help students find language courses abroad.*
Students share their ideas with a partner and then the class.

Exercise 5

Students work in pairs and make two lists about outsourcing. They should base their answers on ideas from the text as well as their own ideas.

Possible answers

Advantages	Disadvantages
• reduces costs	• jobs might be lost
• allows focus on key parts of the business	• less control over all operations and quality
• can result in lower prices for customers	• outsourcing overseas might mean exploitation of labour force
• makes use of outside knowledge/experience	• language difficulties / cultural differences
• improves economy and employment for country with outsourcing	

Exercise 6

▶ 7.1 Students listen, compare their ideas, and complete the table. They may need to listen twice.

Answers
Paula: It's good for developing countries (emerging economies), but it leads to significant job losses at home.
Christian: It frees up resources for core activities, improves efficiency; benefits to economies and infrastructure of country; a way to work with potential markets.
Chitra: The workforce is more flexible, responsive and productive; 24/7 productivity; there are more well-paid jobs, including jobs for women.

EXTRA ACTIVITY
▶ 7.1 For further listening practice, write these questions on the board (answers are shown in brackets). Students listen and answer.

Speaker 1
1 *Where are jobs in these countries going to?*
the UK (India), France (North Africa), Spain (Latin America), Germany (Central Europe – Poland, Hungary), Scandinavia (Baltic States, India)

Speaker 2
2 *How much lower were labour costs?* (70%)
3 *How much of the IT work is in India?* (two-thirds)
4 *How many potential customers do the new markets have?* (hundreds of millions)

Speaker 3
5 *How many hours a day is productivity?* (24/7 – 24 hours a day, seven days a week)
6 *What is the pay like?* (absolutely fantastic)
7 *How much can you make?* (about the same as a junior doctor)

Exercise 7

Students complete the questions with the verbs from the list.

Answers

1 lead to	4 achieve	7 get through
2 develop, create	5 streamline	8 gain
3 take	6 free up	9 improve

Exercise 8

Students take turns to ask and answer the questions in **7**.
They should feel free to reply with ideas from the previous reading and listening. They don't necessarily have to come up with new ideas as long as they are using the vocabulary from this section.

Further practice

If students need more practice, go to *Practice file 7* on page 118 of the *Student's Book*.

Exercise 9

Students read the profile about Company X and consider the advantages and disadvantages for them of outsourcing.

There isn't a definite view on whether this company should outsource, although the opportunities and arguments in favour seem to outweigh those against. However, students should feel free to make up their own minds when preparing to present their ideas.

During feedback, students can comment on which group had the most convincing arguments. Give positive feedback to any group who used plenty of the words/phrases from this section. You could even note which group used the most (see *Extra activity*).

EXTENSION Ask students to think of three things they would like to outsource and share their ideas with a partner, explaining how it would work and what the benefits would be.

Photocopiable worksheet

Download and photocopy *Unit 7 Working with words* worksheet from the teacher resources in the *Online practice*.

Business communication

Exercise 1

Students read the *Context* to find out why Sanjit is visiting, and think about how he might convince GSV Chemicals of why it's a good idea to outsource to Bangalore.

Answer
Sanjit is visiting GSV Chemicals to present his region as a place to outsource.

Exercise 2

▶ **7.2** Students read the questions and listen for the answers. Point out that Sanjit illustrates a good way to structure a presentation.

Answers
1 10,000 companies already based in the region, buoyant labour market, quality of educational institutions, the number of qualified graduates
2 Sanjit asks rhetorical questions to keep attention and he asks the questions he believes his audience want answering. For example: *What does Bangalore have to offer in business terms? How well qualified is the workforce?*

Exercise 3

▶ **7.2** Students read the questions and listen again to identify the phrases used.

Answers
1 Statistics show … / Recent data illustrates …
2 **a** as a result of …
   b due to …

Exercise 4

▶ **7.3** Students listen to the second part of the presentation and answer the questions.

Answers
1 No – Bangalore has a tradition of attracting engineering companies.
2 **a** expected growth in IT services annually
   b multinational software and outsourcing companies that have built offices in Bangalore
   c number of new offices opened in the city in the first four months of this year
   d new staff employed per month
3 Investors will not only obtain a skilled workforce but will also ensure this workforce remains within India.

Exercise 5

Students use the pairs of words to complete the sentences. You could do the first one together. Don't check answers now, as students will listen again in the next exercise to check their answers.

Refer students to the *Tip* for the idiom *food for thought* in sentence 7.

Exercise 6

▶ **7.3** Students listen again to check their answers to **5**.

Answers
1	looked + move	5	looking + see
2	notice + chart	6	look + figures
3	mentioned + earned	7	go + leave
4	turn + attention	8	resulted + changes

Further practice

If students need more practice, go to *Practice file 7* on page 118 of the *Student's Book*.

Exercise 7

Students work in pairs for this activity and can take turns to practise their presentation and use phrases from the *Key expressions*, before presenting to the other pair. With presentations where students work in pairs, it is up to them to decide who will talk about which section.

Allow any students who want to give the whole presentation on their own to do so. In this case, they can rehearse with a partner and then change partners and give a final version.

Students might need help with language for describing the diagrams in section 3 of the chart. Here are some ideas.

a *Looking at this graph, we can see that as you reduce your costs, more money is available for IT investment.*

b *You will notice on this next chart that the reduction in salary costs was a direct result of outsourcing.*

c *Now have a look at how a knock-on effect of outsourcing has been an increase in shareholder value.*

Exercise 8

Students may need to research the topics to feel that they can give a credible presentation. If so, set the task at the end of the lesson and begin the next class with the presentations.

If possible, video the final presentations and set aside time for students to watch and self- or peer-assess their performance.

Photocopiable worksheet

Download and photocopy *Unit 7 Business communication* worksheet from the teacher resources in the *Online practice*.

Practically speaking

Exercise 1

Students read the questions and discuss their opinions with a partner. Elicit one or two comments from the class.

> **Answer**
> 2 Possible reason why people in the audience ask questions or make a comment: to find out information, to check and clarify, to show how much they know, to disagree with the speaker.

Exercise 2

▶ **7.4** Students read the reasons for asking a question, and then listen and answer questions a–d.

> **Answers**
> a 1 b 4 c 2 d 3

Exercise 3

▶ **7.4** Students listen again and write down the three missing words in each sentence.

> **Answers**
> 1 pick up on
> 2 thank you for
> 3 found it useful
> 4 question I have
> 5 show us, again
> 6 talk us through
> 7 make a comment
> 8 comment on that

Point out that it's also a good idea, if you are asked a question and don't know the answer, to say so, and perhaps ask if anyone in the audience knows.

PRONUNCIATION Drill students with these phrases, if necessary, and focus on how they can sound more apologetic by stressing the underlined words in the following phrases.

I do apologize. I'm really sorry.

Discuss this with students before the next activity. Look at the audio script on page 146 of the *Student's Book* together to see the explanations and extra comments the speakers made.

Exercise 4

Students work in groups to give a short presentation. Remind listeners to make notes if necessary to help them ask a question afterwards.

Give feedback on how they ask questions, as well as on how well the speaker deals with the questions.

PRE-WORK LEARNERS Students can choose a topic related to their studies.

Language at work

Exercise 1

This opening grammar point should be a review and a quick check of students' understanding.

> **Answers**
> 1 passive – The speaker wishes to emphasize the *thousands of jobs*. The jobs have been outsourced by companies but in this context, it is not important which ones.
> 2 active – The focus of the speaker is that the EU companies have done this action.

Exercise 2

Students underline the passive form in each sentence.

> **Answers**
> 1 Bangalore's educational institutions <u>have</u> <u>been</u> <u>awarded</u> international recognition by a number of organizations.
> 2 It <u>is</u> <u>said</u> that Indian IT services will continue to grow over the next five years.
> 3 The arguments for outsourcing <u>weren't</u> <u>presented</u> convincingly enough.
> 4 Next, the call <u>is</u> automatically <u>transferred</u> overseas to a call centre in Bangalore.

Exercise 3

Students match the sentences in **2** to the categories in the *Language point*.

> **Answers**
> a 1 b 4 c 3 d 2

Grammar reference

If students need more information, go to *Grammar reference* on page 119 of the *Student's Book*.

Exercise 4

Students read the question and the sentences, and change the ones that would sound more natural in the passive form. Encourage them to explain why. You could do the first one together.

Answers
1 This sounds better in the passive because we are not interested in *who*, but the fact that it is stored somewhere: *A lot of our sensitive information is stored in secure remote sites.*
2 The speaker is interested in *who*, so the active form is appropriate.
3 The speaker can't believe that no one knows where Jason is, so the active form is natural.
4 Again, the person or agent in this sentence is not important to the listener, so the passive should be used: *The road has been closed for repairs for two weeks.*
5 The first clause sounds natural in the active, but the second clause doesn't need to refer to who is doing the action: *You can't use the lift today because it is being serviced.*

Exercise 5

Students rephrase the sentences using the passive to avoid saying who is responsible.

Answers
1 The decision has been made …
2 the photocopier hasn't been fixed yet.
3 The package was sent (from the post room) yesterday …
4 they are being made …
5 your complaint will be dealt with.

Exercise 6

The passive can be used to hide the name of a person. It is often used with bad news or where a mistake has been made. The following phrases are often used in this context.
It is said …, It is known …, It is thought …, It is believed …, It is expected …
Students use the passive to make the sentences less personal.

Answers
1 It is said that Singapore's very nice …
2 It is known that Indian software engineers are …
3 It is thought that property in London is …
4 It is believed that Microsoft is interested in …
5 It is expected that outsourcing overseas will …

Further practice
If students need more practice, go to *Practice file 7* on page 119 of the *Student's Book*.

Exercise 7

Students work in pairs to discuss a recent work or news story.

Give feedback on both the active and the passive. The danger is that students will try to overuse the passive. Remind them that, in the majority of cases, the active is the better option as it is more direct and clear.

Photocopiable worksheet
Download and photocopy *Unit 7 Language at work* worksheet from the teacher resources in the *Online practice*.

Talking point

Discussion

Exercise 1

Students discuss the question. Elicit some of their ideas.

PRE-WORK LEARNERS Ask students to consider how some of the work done at their college could be done by robots. They could also consider the main industry / biggest company in their home town. Students could then talk about the same industry in **2**, and later in the *Task*, exercise **1**.

Exercise 2

Students consider how the industry they work in may be affected in the future.

Exercise 3

Students read the questions and then read the text. Ask them to discuss their answers with a partner.

Answers
Companies may be able to save 90% of employee costs by using robots.
Other considerations could include: employee motivation; staff welfare; customer preferences; the customer experience

Task

Exercise 1

Students read the questions on the right of the text, answer them individually, and then discuss their conclusions in pairs. Extend the discussion to the whole class to see whether students agree with the results, and why.

Exercise 2

Students work in groups of four, in two pairs of two. Give them five to seven minutes to draw up a list of arguments.

ONE-TO-ONE One of you takes the role of a manager, and the other one an employee. Individually, draw up a list of reasons and use your arguments in discussion with each other in **3**.

Exercise 3

Students present their arguments to the other pair. Encourage each pair to negotiate and to accept some ideas to try to reach an agreement.

When each group is ready, compare answers and find out what issues they agreed on.

Progress test
Download and photocopy *Unit 7 Progress test* and *Speaking test* from the teacher resources in the *Online practice*.

8 Employees

Context

The days when employees were seen as disposable and replaceable have ended in many businesses. Employees are the company's most important resource. With more staff needing to be employed and possibly trained for highly-skilled positions, it is expensive for companies to lose staff. At the same time, with many countries introducing measures to encourage greater fluidity within the labour market, companies are more willing to hire on a freelance basis and more employees are keen to sell their expertise to the highest bidders.

Companies must therefore work harder to retain good staff. They might use benefits and incentives, as a good wage or salary might not be enough to keep an employee. Companies will need to offer yearly appraisals to plan a strategy of professional development with members of staff to ensure they feel they have career ambitions which can be met within the limits of the company.

In the first section of this unit, students will discuss some of the issues arising from these points – the major one for a company being how to retain staff and avoid high staff turnover. The communication skill of negotiating is normally considered to be about buying and selling, but the context in this unit – an internal situation where managers need to redeploy existing staff – highlights students' need for negotiating skills in all areas of business. To support the language of negotiating, students review and practise first and second conditionals. In the *Talking point*, they consider how challenging jobs are in the light of a design diagram, with the aim of achieving true job satisfaction.

Starting point
Students discuss these questions. Encourage them to give examples from their own experience of work, or people they know.

Possible answers
1 Employees leave a company for a better job, better pay, to take a career break, etc.
2 An employer can encourage them to stay by offering more money, promotion, diversity, company shares, etc.

Working with words

Exercise 1
Students read the questions and discuss their ideas with a partner. Elicit some of their ideas.

Exercise 2
Students read the questions and then read the text to find the answers. They can check their answers with a partner.

Check students understand *apprentice* – a young person who works for an employer for a fixed period of time in order to learn the particular skills needed in their job – and *to sink in* – to be fully understood or realized.

Answers
1 The owners gave the company to the staff.
2 They couldn't think of better owners than the employees.
3 As an employee-ownership trust with an operational board.
4 Because it's their own business.

Exercise 3
Encourage students to consider different businesses or industries, e.g. their own or one they know; a university; a department store; a factory, etc. They could work in small groups to do this. Elicit some of their ideas.

Exercise 4
Students work in pairs to find the verb forms in the article. You could suggest they underline them. Then ask them to look at the other forms of *employ*, and do the same.

Answers
In the text:
employee (person n) – person who works for a company
employer (person n) – person who employs people
employed (past participle verb – passive form) – when you have a job
employment (n) – refers to the situation of having or providing jobs
Other forms:
self-employed (adj) – when you work for yourself
unemployed (adj) – when you have no job
employable (adj) – when someone has the potential to get a job
unemployable (adj) – when someone can't be employed for certain reasons
employability (adj) – whether someone could get a job
unemployment (n) – refers to the situation of not having a job

Exercise 5

You could allocate one or two words to each pair, then ask them to check their ideas with another pair before checking the answers as a group. They could also check their answers in a dictionary.

Answers
apprentices (person n) – young people who work for a company and learn on-the-job
apprenticeship (n) – a programme run by a company to employ and teach a young person a skill
retirement (n) – when an older person (usually in their sixties) finishes working and lives on a pension
profitable (adj) – when a business makes money
owner (person n) – person who owns/has a business
operational (adj) – something which is functioning/working
management (n) – the people in a company who are in charge of the staff and the general running of the company

Exercise 6

Students read the questions and discuss their ideas with a partner. Encourage them to use the words from **4** and **5**. Remind students that we say 'It depends,' or 'It depends on (something/someone) …' and then list a few ideas.

> **DICTIONARY SKILLS**
>
> Brainstorm vocabulary for referring to different stages of training and employment, e.g. *employee, apprentice, trainee, manager, leader, retiree, owner*, etc.
>
> Ask students to use their dictionaries to check the meanings and differences between these words. Then ask students to work in pairs and to draw a mind map, showing links between the words. Students then compare mind maps with another pair and explain to each other why they grouped and linked the words in the way they did.

Exercise 7

▶ **8.1** Students will hear two employees talking about their employment history. They should read the questions and then listen to find the answers.

Check students understand *redundancy money* – the money somebody receives when they have to leave their job because there is no more work available to them. You could elicit a definition and/or an example.

Answers
Speaker 1
1 working in a car factory and now an IT consultant
2 He was made redundant.
3 He did more training.
Speaker 2
1 because of no opportunity for advancement
2 by making her a manager of the new office
3 It's hardly ever about money. It's about ambition, job satisfaction, growth opportunities and personal development.

Exercise 8

Students turn to audio script 8.1 on page 146 of the *Student's Book* and find the pairs of phrases. They should work with a partner to explain the difference in meaning between them. Do the first one together.

Answers
1 *Career prospects* refer to future opportunities in general within an area of business – not just a job but also promotion, etc. *Job opportunities* refers to specific jobs only.
2 *Full-time employment* means you have a paid job for working 35 hours a week (or more). An *apprenticeship* is when you learn on-the-job and are paid less than a normal employee.
3 *Job security* refers to if your job is safe from redundancy, etc. *Job satisfaction* refers to the enjoyment and rewards of doing it.
4 *Taking early retirement* is voluntary, and also means finishing work for good. *Being made redundant* is not voluntary, can happen at any time, and the person usually hopes to go back to work.
5 *Relocate* is to move for a job. *Redeploy* means you are moved by the company.
6 *Being laid off* is the action of the company to employees (because there isn't enough work). *Being unemployed* (having no job to go to) is the result.
7 *A sideways move* means the person may be in a different part of the company or have a different job, but there is no progress or development. *A change of direction* will bring new opportunities.
8 *A glass ceiling* refers to the limit in a company you can reach in terms of advancement. In other words, you can see higher positions above you, but you will never be able to move into these for reasons such as gender. *An opportunity for advancement* means you have a chance to move up in the company.
9 *Training* is a formal situation where a 'trainer' works with employees. *Personal development* refers to broader ways of learning and developing; for example, being assigned new responsibilities, reading a trade journal or attending a conference will all help the employee 'develop'.

> **EXTRA ACTIVITY**
>
> ▶ **8.1** Ask students to listen again and think of someone they know who is similar to one of the people talking. Ask them to look at the audio script, and highlight phrases they could 'steal' or use to talk about the person they know, e.g. 'without any qualifications'; 'there wasn't a lot of opportunity for advancement'.
>
> Students then work in pairs and tell each other about their familiar person, using the phrases. Students listening should ask questions to find out any similar or different aspects.

Further practice

If students need more practice, go to *Practice file 8* on page 120 of the *Student's Book*.

Exercise 9

Students work in pairs. They read the questions and tell each other about a job change. Encourage them to use the words and phrases from **4, 5** and **8**. Give feedback on good use of vocabulary and phrases.

PRE-WORK LEARNERS Students could discuss any work experience or part-time jobs they have had, or talk about someone they know well.

Exercise 10

Students discuss the three statements. To help students prepare their ideas and opinions, you could draw this table on the board for them to copy.

	Arguments for	*Arguments against*	*Examples*
Statement 1			
Statement 2			
Statement 3			

As students discuss each statement, they can complete the table with the arguments for and against. This will help ensure a balanced discussion before students come to a final opinion to present to the class. In the third column, students can make notes on relevant examples given from the group. (This column could be left out with pre-work learners.)

Photocopiable worksheet
Download and photocopy *Unit 8 Working with words* worksheet from the teacher resources in the *Online practice*.

Business communication

Exercise 1

Students read the questions and bullet point situations. In pairs, they discuss which ones they are involved in and explain who else is involved. Elicit one or two ideas from them.

PRE-WORK LEARNERS Ask students to consider the following situations: (at school/college) when you can hand in an assignment; missing a class / seminar / lecture; working with other students on projects.

Exercise 2

Before playing the listening, ask students to read the *Context* and briefly comment on what thoughts Dermot and Johanna might have before the meeting starts. The likelihood is that both will be keen to avoid losing any good members of their existing staff to the new team. For this reason, there may be a conflict of interests at the meeting.

▶ **8.2** Students read the three questions before listening.

Answers
1 the other two teams would lose their most capable people
2 three people from each team
3 contract workers get paid more and it's bad for team spirit

Exercise 3

▶ **8.2** Students read the expressions 1–10 and then listen to find out who said them. You could ask students, first, if they can remember who said which expression. Students can also find the phrases in the *Key expressions* and make a note of the functional use of each phrase.

Answers
1 J   2 D   3 J   4 J   5 D   6 D   7 J   8 J   9 D   10 J

Refer students to the *Tip*. Using *What* at the beginning of a sentence is useful when putting forward a proposal.

Exercise 4

▶ **8.3** Refer students to the hand-written notes. Ask them to read them. Students then listen to the second part of the meeting and correct the notes Johanna made.

Answers
<u>Three</u> people to be transferred …
Brett <u>can't be expected</u> to do the trainees' work.
Timo <u>won't join</u> the new team. (Sabrina will go instead.)
Deadline from HR = <u>before</u> <u>Friday</u>
Students might also decide to add the following to the notes:
Lena and Marlon will also go from Johanna's team.
Jamie and Pascale will also go from Dermot's team.

Exercise 5

▶ **8.3** Ask students to read the sentences. Then play the listening and ask them to put them in the order in which they hear them.

Answers
1 *Let's just summarize the situation.*
2 I could offer you three, but I'd expect three from your team, too.
3 If you guaranteed Brett, I'd let you have Jamie, Pascal and Timo.
4 I'll be happy for Brett to be on the team, provided you replace one of the trainees with someone experienced.
5 Unless we get this list to HR before Friday, we won't be sending anyone.
6 So, a quick recap: if I send Brett …, you'll send Sabrina …
7 I can live with that.
8 *That sounds like a plan.*

PRONUNCIATION Ask students to find one phrase in each group in the *Key expressions* which they would like to use, and to underline the stressed word(s) in each one, e.g. *What we need to decide on <u>today</u> is …; One option would be to …; I can <u>live</u> with that.* Tell them to compare phrases with a partner and then practise saying them out loud to each other. They will then be able to use these more effectively in **6** and **7**.

Further practice
If students need more practice, go to *Practice file 8* on page 120 of the *Student's Book*.

If students need more practice of the phrases before doing **6** and **7**, especially the bargaining phrases, write the following situations on the board for them to role-play in A/B pairs.

You both work on reception. A wants to do some shopping at lunchtime so needs 30 minutes extra. Negotiate with B for him/her to work longer today and answer the phones.

You both share one TV. B wants to watch football (for 90 minutes), but A's favourite programme is on for 30 minutes on the other channel during the second half of the match. Negotiate a solution.

Give feedback on the use of the phrases only. As these are quite short and fun, some pairs could perform their negotiation for the rest of the class.

Exercise 6

Students read the situation. To begin with, they could study the headings under *Key expressions* and check they know the phrases to use with each stage. Then, in pairs, they structure how the negotiation could proceed. They will need to think about the negotiating position of both the employer and employee and what to ask for at each stage of the negotiation. Unlike other role-plays, this activity lets students add more of their own ideas and demands. Once they are happy with their structure, they can decide which role to take and carry out the negotiation. Afterwards, ask students to say what they received in the negotiation. Find out which employee and employer got the best deal.

ALTERNATIVE Put all the employees together in one group and all the employers in another group to discuss together first what they would like to achieve in the negotiation. Then students pair up and negotiate.

Exercise 7

Students work in groups of four. Each pair turns to the page indicated to read and prepare for a negotiation between managers and their employees who are thinking of leaving to join a competitor with better working conditions. Managers have to negotiate a series of incentives to retain the employees. Allow time for preparation beforehand as well as time at the end for pairs to report their results to the class.

Listen in and make notes of the negotiating expressions. Afterwards, ask students first if they think their negotiation was successful, and why. Groups could compare their outcomes with each other. Give feedback on use of the negotiating expressions, in particular, using the correct ones at each stage.

ONE-TO-ONE For this activity, the teacher and student take a different role each. You could do the role-play activity twice, swapping roles the second time.

Photocopiable worksheet

Download and photocopy *Unit 8 Business communication* worksheet from the teacher resources in the *Online practice*.

Practically speaking

Exercise 1

Students discuss the questions with a partner, and then you can share and compare a few ideas with the class.

Exercise 2

▶ 8.4 Students listen and identify what help is requested in the six conversations.

In 6, *roster* means timetable or schedule.

Answers
The first speaker wants the other person to
1 answer a survey
2 help with a computer
3 check an email
4 help with the photocopier
5 look at some figures
6 help with the holiday roster
Speaker 2 agrees to help in 1, 4, 5 and 6 (though not immediately).

Exercise 3

▶ 8.4 Students listen for the responses and replies.

Answers
1 Yeah, sure. (Oh, thanks a lot.)
2 Sorry, I'm a bit busy right now. (Oh, well, never mind.)
3 Sorry, I'm just on my way to a client's. (OK, it's not that urgent.)
4 Give me two minutes and I'll be right with you. (Thanks.)
5 Certainly. Take a seat. (Thanks.)
6 Sorry, no time! … I'll look at it later. (OK.)

Exercise 4

Students categorize the requests in **3**. Some of the requests are neutral and will be appropriate in most situations.

Suggested answers
M: 3, 4, 5   L: 1, 2, 6

Exercise 5

Students practise the phrases with the situations. The phrases will be determined by the formality of the situation.

Language at work

Exercise 1

Students read about the 'IF triangle' and answer the questions.

Answers
It's called the 'IF triangle' because it's useful to start sentences in negotiations with 'if' and we normally negotiate about things related to time, cost and quality. Negotiating on one or two of these will always affect the other.

Exercise 2

Students read the sentences and decide which types of issue they are negotiating in each case.

Answers
a time and cost
b quality, time and cost
c time and cost
d cost and quality

Exercise 3

▶ **8.5** Students read the words, then listen to the four sentences in **2**, and for the words which can be replaced. You may need to play the listening twice.

> **Answers**
> They replace *if*, or *if not* in the case of *unless*.

Exercise 4

Students read the *Language point*, answer the questions and match the phrases.

> **Answers**
> 1 high possibility – **a, b**; more imaginary – **c, d**
> 2 **a** and **b** = first conditional (*if* + present tense / *will* + infinitive)
>   **c** and **d** = second conditional (*if* + past tense / *would* + infinitive)
> 3 **a** unless **b** provided **c** supposing **d** in case

Grammar reference
If students need more information, go to *Grammar reference* on page 121 of the *Student's Book*.

Exercise 5

Students have already come across these alternatives to the word *if* in the phrases from the previous section.

Note that in sentences 2, 4 and 5, students are offered two options to make sentences with. In 5, the phrase *as long as* meaning 'on condition that' is given.

> **Possible answers**
> 1 you pay in cash
> 2 (unless) you pay extra / (in case) there's a delay
> 3 you be interested then
> 4 (Unless …) you won't be eligible for the special offer / (Provided that …) we can give you a lower price
> 5 (in case) you have any problems / (as long as) you use this number
> 6 would you be able to do mine next month

Further practice
If students need more practice, go to *Practice file 8* on page 121 of the *Student's Book*.

Exercise 6

Students study the situation between the manager and the employee on page 137 of the *Student's Book*. They use conditionals to weigh up the different options and outcomes. Once they have worked through all the items and prepared arguments, they role-play the situation. Afterwards, pairs can comment on and compare the final agreement.

Listen for and make comments on use of conditionals and the linking words. Note that in speech it is often unrealistic and unnatural to use a full two-clause conditional sentence. Students will tend to use parts of the full sentence.

Photocopiable worksheet
Download and photocopy *Unit 8 Language at work* worksheet from the teacher resources in the *Online practice*.

Talking point

Discussion

Exercise 1

Students read the questions and discuss their answers with a partner. Check *staff retention* = keeping ('retaining') staff. This question should work well with students from the same, or a different company.

PRE-WORK LEARNERS Ask students to consider a company they know well, or perhaps one where there have recently been employee changes or redundancies, and to think about why.

Exercise 2

Brainstorm one or two ideas as a whole class, e.g. *make expectations clear; involve staff in decision-making,* before asking students to continue adding to the list in pairs. Students then read the text to compare their ideas.

Exercise 3

Students discuss the questions in pairs. Encourage them to share any experiences they have had.

EXTENSION Ask students whether employees should be allowed to take the initiative to keep themselves motivated and challenged at work, and how. Encourage them to share any examples they know of.

Task

Exercise 1

Students work in pairs. They read about the employees, discuss the situation and match them to a face in the diagram.

> **Suggested answers**
> **Ryan:** boredom
> **Susan:** anxiety
> **Ian:** flow

Exercise 2

Students first work on their own to list tasks they regularly do. They should then decide where on the diagram each task goes, based on skill and difficulty levels. In pairs, they can compare and discuss the tasks and how they feel about them.

PRE-WORK LEARNERS Ask students to think about any tasks they have been involved in during part-time employment, or any tasks they know about that friends or colleagues do. They can use these to place on the diagram.

Exercise 3

Students compare and discuss the tasks, and how they feel about each one, with a partner. Listeners should be ready to offer advice and suggestions if any of the tasks are not challenging enough!

Progress test
Download and photocopy *Unit 8 Progress test* and *Speaking test* from the teacher resources in the *Online practice*.

9 New business

Unit content

By the end of this unit, students will be able to
- talk about start-ups
- ask contacts for help and avoid saying 'no'
- talk about past or recent activities and results.

Context

Many people, possibly including some of your students, would like to start their own new business. Perhaps they have a good business idea and they are attracted to the idea of working alone. Their motivation might be to make more money by running their own company and therefore improve their lifestyle. However, very few of these people will ever get past the thinking stage and of those that do, the vast majority of businesses close down within their first year of trading.

Lack of planning is one key reason why new businesses fail. A good idea is not enough. Writing a business plan will help prepare for all aspects of the business from marketing to financing. This document is also needed if a future entrepreneur is to attract any kind of investment from banks or business angels (investors).

You also have to convince such people that you can do something the competition is unable to. Very few new business ideas are completely new and there's always someone else doing something similar, or a company which will copy your idea very quickly once it's launched. In addition, competition for new business is increasingly coming from overseas, as companies can 'go global' much more quickly nowadays through selling overseas via websites.

In this unit, students begin by hearing interviews with successful owners of business start-ups who mention some of the issues above. In *Business communication*, students practise the language for asking about work and life, along with the tricky skill of asking a favour and politely saying 'no'. Finally, in the *Talking point*, students consider a different approach to selling products or services to be able to compete with new online businesses.

Starting point

Discuss these questions as a class. Even students with no experience of business start-ups should be able to guess at answers for questions 1 and 2.

Possible answers

1 Because they have a good business idea, they want to be their own boss, they want the challenge, etc.
2 Lack of money, lack of knowledge and skills, competing with existing and established businesses, etc.
3 Such people are usually described as dynamic and highly motivated and with a vision. However, the common feature of all entrepreneurs is that they are hard workers and are willing to work very long days for no financial reward at the beginning.

Working with words

Exercise 1

Students can discuss their ideas with a partner.

Possible answers

Do market research and test the idea out on family, friends and different people.

Exercise 2

At this stage, students only read the title of the article. Elicit some of their ideas.

Answers

start-up – connected with starting a new business or project
pop-up – a temporary/mobile stand or space at an event or in a place with many people, which sells, promotes or advertises goods or services

Exercise 3

Students read the four questions and then read the text again to find the answers. They can check their ideas with a partner.

Check the meaning and word stress of *relying* (*to rely on someone; reliable*).

Answers

1 by asking them to throw their empty cups into bins marked 'Yes' and 'No'
2 through a fund called 'Jam Jar Investments'
3 cost-effective way to test the market for a new product and helps generate initial revenue to go towards start-up costs
4 somewhere with crowds, e.g. an event like a football match or concert, or in an empty shop on the high street

Exercise 4

Students discuss their answers with a partner. Elicit a few ideas of why this might work, or not, in their business.

PRE-WORK LEARNERS Ask students to think of a business they know something about, and why the pop-up idea would or wouldn't work.

EXTENSION If students can think of a business where the pop-up idea would work, ask them to think of two things that could be done on a pop-up stand to encourage active involvement from customers.

Exercise 5

Students match the words in bold in the article to their definitions 1–11.

Answers

1	financial backing	7	to turn over
2	start-up capital	8	a gap in the market
3	temporary outlet (pop-up stall)	9	pop-up stall
4	would-be entrepreneurs	10	venture capitalist
5	business model	11	return on investment
6	investment fund		

Exercise 6

Students read the text and complete it with words from **5**.

Answers

1	entrepreneur	5	fund
2	market	6	backing
3	capital	7	outlet
4	model	8	investment

Exercise 7

▶ **9.1** Students read the category headings and then take notes on what James Murray Wells says.

Answers

Type of business: Glasses Direct sells glasses and contact lenses online, at a fraction of the price you pay if you go to a high street optician.
Start-up finance: A loan from his parents.
Biggest challenge: Getting the manufacturers to work with him.
Marketing: Pop-up events
Advice: 'if you've got a sound business model and you see a gap in the market, go for it.'

Exercise 8

▶ **9.2** Students listen to the extracts and write down the adjectives they hear.

Answers

1	outrageous	4	helpful
2	important	5	difficult
3	fantastic	6	ridiculous

PRONUNCIATION Note that we often stress these types of adverbs in sentences to add emphasis. For example:

That's extremely kind of you!

It's a really profitable business.

To practise, write these two example sentences on the board and drill them with the stress. In exercise **10**, encourage students to stress the adverb in their responses.

Exercise 9

Students read the *Tip* on gradable and ungradable adjectives. They then read the two questions and find the answers by referring to **8**.

Answers

1 very, extremely, incredibly
2 completely, absolutely, totally

Exercise 10

Students think of ways to respond to the situations.

You could organize this so that, in pairs, one student reads statements 1–5. The other student keeps the book closed and listens and responds.

Suggested answers

1 That's totally outrageous!
2 It can be extremely risky.
3 That's absolutely fantastic!
4 That must be really worrying for you.
5 That's incredibly high.

Further practice

If students need more practice, go to *Practice file 9* on page 122 of the *Student's Book*.

Exercise 11

Students read the two business ideas (or think of their own). For question 1, encourage students to respond with an adverb + adjective combination. Groups could make notes on their discussion for each question and compare answers with the rest of the class afterwards.

Comment on the use of the vocabulary from **5** as well as the use of adverbs + adjectives. Make sure students stress the adverbs so that their intonation doesn't sound too flat.

Possible answers

2 They might need help with finance and start-up capital. As well as approaching business angels or investors, they might be able to get funding from local councils / government departments who are keen to sponsor initiatives for reducing congestion.
3 Previous schemes to encourage road users and commuters to give up their own private transport have not been wholly successful. People prefer the independence and comfort of cars. The PIN number cars may offer the users comfort but the scooters are likely to attract only a niche market, in the same way that some people take collapsible bicycles to work. In addition to this, people will only ride scooters in good weather.

Photocopiable worksheet

Download and photocopy *Unit 9 Working with words* worksheet from the teacher resources in the *Online practice*.

Business communication

Exercise 1

To discuss this lead-in question, students don't necessarily have to mention someone they met in a work-related or business situation. It could be an old school friend or distant relative they hadn't seen for years.

Exercise 2

▶ 9.3 Before playing the listening, give students time to read the *Context* and familiarize themselves with the contents of the table. They then listen to three conversations. You might need to play the listening twice for students to complete the entire table. Tell them that the background noises will help them identify the situation in conversation 3.

Answers
Conversation 1: A phone call at work / Ex-work colleagues / Had a promotion / New local member of staff
Conversation 2: At an airport / College friends / Works in car industry / Business contacts
Conversation 3: In a coffee shop / Business acquaintances / Business has lost customers / Contacts in Internet insurance business

Exercise 3

Students may find it helpful to listen again. Also ask them to make a note of any phrases which tell them if the conversation is more or less formal, e.g. *What are you doing here?* (less formal in conversation 2) and *Thank you for finding the time to meet* (more formal in conversation 3).

Answers
a 3 **b** 1 **c** 2

Exercise 4

Students can do this exercise in pairs.

Exercise 5

▶ 9.3 Students listen to the first conversation again and check their answers.

Answers
1 h **2** e **3** f **4** a **5** g **6** c **7** b **8** d

Exercise 6

Students categorize the phrases. They can check their answers in the *Key expressions*.

Answers
a I'm not sure if you remember me. / I haven't seen you for ages. / It's good to hear from you.
b What have you been doing? / How's work?
c That's actually the reason why I'm calling.
d The thing is, I'm looking for someone to work with us …
e I'll certainly think about it.

Exercise 7

Students identify the phrases in conversations 2 and 3 in audio script 9.3 on page 148 of the *Student's Book* and then compare the phrases used in all three conversations.
Refer students to the *Tip* on *anyway*.

Answers
Conversation 2
a What are you doing here? / When was the last time we saw each other?
b What about you? / What have you been up to? / Are you still working in …?
c By the way, could you do me a favour?
d Could you put me in touch with …?
e Let's chat about that over dinner.
Conversation 3
a Good morning … Thank you for finding the time to meet. / It's been a long time since we've been in contact.
b How's life treating you? / How's business with you? / What's been happening?
c And with that in mind, maybe I could ask you for a favour.
d We are looking for … and I wondered if ….
e It sounds an interesting proposal. / Send me the details. / I can't promise anything, though!

EXTRA ACTIVITY
Now that students have focused on the phrases, they will need plenty of practice in using the language. In **8**, they will have two conversations. However, for more controlled practice, ask students to work in pairs and look back at the table in **2**. There are two extra pieces of information which are unused under each heading. Students can combine one piece of information from under each heading to write a short conversation between two people. For example, the conversation might take place in a taxi queue between a customer and a supplier, one of whom has recently married a French person. The supplier is looking for venture capital to start up on his/her own. Students write their A/B conversations using phrases from the section and perform them to the class or to other pairs of students.

Further practice

If students need more practice, go to *Practice file 9* on page 122 of the *Student's Book*.

Exercise 8

Students use the flow chart to have the two conversations. Tell them to agree whether the conversations will be more formal or not.

Give feedback on use of the *Key expressions*, but also focus on register and the level of formality. Make sure that students aren't mixing phrases with different formality or meaning. For example, if A begins by saying *Thank you for finding the time to meet me*, it will sound strange for B to reply with a phrase such as *I haven't seen you for ages!*

ALTERNATIVE Ask students to work in pairs and to choose one or two phrases from each group in the *Key expressions* which they would like to use. They should take a slip of paper for each phrase and write down just one word to act as a prompt for the whole phrase. They should decide on which word together, e.g. for *I'm not sure if you remember me*, they could write down **sure**; and for *What have you been up to?*, **up**.

Exercise 9

This is a fun way to end this section. Students write true events but also create untrue information. They both attempt to guess what is true/untrue at the end of the conversation.

Photocopiable worksheet
Download and photocopy *Unit 9 Business communication* worksheet from the teacher resources in the *Online practice*.

Practically speaking

Exercise 1

Students read and discuss the questions with a partner. Elicit some ideas about their experiences.

The issue of avoiding saying 'no' is both a question of someone's personality and also of their national or business culture. For example, we can feel uncomfortable saying 'no' to a friend or colleague. And for some nationalities, saying 'no' immediately is considered impolite. Discuss these issues openly with your students.

> **Possible answers**
> It often depends on how well you know the other person or what kind of culture they come from. Some cultures actively avoid using the word 'no' and would find it impolite and too direct. Others prefer a direct 'no'.

Exercise 2

▶ **9.4** Students read the expressions and then listen to three people making requests and tick the ones they hear.

> **Answers**
> I'd love to help, but I think I'm away …
> You know I'd normally help, but at the moment …
> I'm afraid I don't have any spare time …
> Try me again in a few months' time.

PRONUNCIATION Play the listening again and ask students to focus on how these phrases in **2** were used. Ask them to underline the stressed words and consider whether the intonation is flat, or goes up or down in places. Then ask them what phrases they would use in their own language, which words are stressed and what happens to the intonation. Note that when we are trying to be polite, and apologize for saying 'no' in English, we usually stress key words and use a wider intonation.

> **Answers**
> I'd <u>love</u> to help, but I think I'm away …
> You know I'd <u>normally</u> help, but at the <u>moment</u> …
> I'm afraid I don't have <u>any</u> spare time …
> <u>Try</u> me again in a <u>few</u> months' time.

Exercise 3

Students work in pairs. They read the situations, and in turn make a request, and respond. If you have an odd number of students, you could ask one student to listen in and tick off any appropriate phrases they hear.

Give feedback on use of phrases and appropriate excuses.

> **EXTRA ACTIVITY**
> Students work in pairs and think of two other request situations. They then join with another pair and make the request. Each person in the other pair should come up with an excuse. Find out what is the best excuse!

Language at work

Exercise 1

This exercise should be revision for students. They underline and identify the tense in each sentence.

> **Answers**
> 1 has secured – present perfect simple
> 2 have been keeping – present perfect continuous
> 3 has been – present perfect simple
> 4 have been commuting – present perfect continuous
> 5 has lived – present perfect simple

Exercise 2

Students read the *Language point* and match sentences 1, 2 and 3 from **1** to situations a–c, then answer questions d and e.

> **Answers**
> a sentence 2 – present perfect continuous
> b sentence 3 – present perfect simple
> c sentence 1 – present perfect simple
> d The present perfect continuous suggests something is temporary.
> e *For* refers to a period of time (*for years*); *since* refers to a specific moment in time (*since last month*).

Grammar reference
If students need more information, go to *Grammar reference* on page 123 of the *Student's Book*.

Exercise 3

Students read the sentence halves and match each with a suitable alternative, a or b. Students can check their answers with a partner. Be sure they can explain, in each case, why the tense is used. You could do the first one together.

> **Answers**
> 1 I've worked out a final price – b (It is finished and the speaker has made final conclusions.)
> I've been working out a final price – a (This is unfinished.)
> 2 I've been calling Mrs Fischer – a (The situation is unfinished. Presumably the speaker has to keep calling.)
> I've called Mrs Fischer – b (The speaker won't call again because he/she has left a message.)
> 3 I've worked with Karen – b (This is permanent.)
> I've been working with Karen – a (This is temporary.)
> 4 We've been hiring – b (This emphasizes the activity.)
> We've hired – a (This emphasizes the result.)

Further practice
If students need more practice, go to *Practice file 9* on page 123 of the *Student's Book*.

Exercise 4

Students write a second part for each pair of sentence starters in an appropriate way. They then read their sentences. Be sure they differentiate between the two tenses clearly. Elicit a few examples of sentence pairs from the group.

Exercise 5

Students work in pairs and take turns to ask and answer questions about their information, using the present perfect simple or continuous. Note that the student answering should use the simple form if the task has/hasn't been done, but the continuous form if it is ongoing.

Exercise 6

Allow about five minutes for students to think about what the project is, what it includes and perhaps also who is involved.

Focus feedback on content, i.e. the activities they talk about, for example, if they are particularly innovative or different; encourage other students to comment, too. Give feedback also on language: this will be on the correct use of form and use of the two tenses. You could put any incorrect forms on the board for whole-class correction.

PRE-WORK LEARNERS Students could consider a real or imaginary project at their place of study, or describe a project of a company they know well or one they've read about in the newspaper or on the Internet. If necessary, they could research this before the next lesson.

Photocopiable worksheet
Download and photocopy *Unit 9 Language at work* worksheet from the teacher resources in the *Online practice*.

Talking point

Discussion

Exercise 1

▶ **9.5** Students read the question and then listen to part of the lecture using the diagram.

> **Answer**
> The 'head' represents mass-market products. The 'long tail' represents niche products that continue to sell over long periods of time.

Exercise 2

Students discuss the question with a partner.

> **Possible answers**
> Online music streaming services can offer far more titles and songs than retail high street shops. So, while both retail and online shops may sell a similar quantity of 'popular' goods (head), an online company can also offer less well-known, niche songs (long tail). Rhapsody is an American company, and an example of this.

Exercise 3

Students discuss the question with a partner.

EXTENSION Ask students whether their business, or another company they know, has the potential to sell 'long tail' products. If so, is it likely that the company will become more profitable as a result? Keep the discussions brief, so as not to pre-empt **3** in the *Task*.

Task

Exercise 1

Students work in groups of four. They read the profiles of three small businesses and then discuss the products or services of each one.

ONE-TO-ONE Ask your student to choose one of the small businesses and prepare their ideas, while you take another. Alternatively, you could brainstorm ideas together for one of the businesses.

Exercise 2

Students join another group to present and compare their ideas.

Exercise 3

Students now think about their own company, and read and answer the questions.

PRE-WORK LEARNERS Ask students to consider how their school or college operates as a company, and whether it has products or services which are part of the 'head' or part of a 'long tail'. For example, the college could offer face-to-face classes, but also online distance learning where classes take place at a time to suit the students (e.g. recordings of lectures, downloadable reading tasks, etc.). Alternatively, students could share information about a company whose products and services they know.

Exercise 4

Ask one person from each group to present their ideas from **3** to the rest of the class.

Progress test
Download and photocopy *Unit 9 Progress test* and *Speaking test* from the teacher resources in the *Online practice*.

Viewpoint 3

Preview

The topic of this *Viewpoint* is *Entrepreneurs*. Students begin by considering what types of people start their own business. They then watch a video about someone who set up their own business, before watching an extended interview with an expert in entrepreneurship, in which they learn about how this is done. Finally, they prepare and give a short presentation on how to become an entrepreneur.

Exercise 1

Students first work individually, and then share their words with the group. Encourage them to give reasons or examples for their choice of words.

ALTERNATIVE If you have access to the Internet in class, you could use an online tool to bring up a word cloud: get students to type in their words and then click to see which words occur most often: those will be in a bigger font.

EXTENSION Find out briefly if the students know anyone who has started their own business: what sort of people are they? Was/Is the business successful?

Exercise 2

▶ **01** Give students time to read the six categories and then play the video, asking them to take notes. Students can compare answers in pairs.

Exercise 3

▶ **01** Students compare the information they wrote down, and add more details. They then watch the video again to check their notes.

Answers
1 because she served *bolitas* to everybody and thought 'why not?' (set up a business) and serve them to other people
2 the gap is for healthy snacks
3 a savoury thing to eat with coffee; the national snack of Brazil
4 because she sells them to coffee shops, leisure centres and Christmas markets; people are more aware of them
5 a loan from the bank and from her own money
6 getting the product to market (marketing) and taking them to coffee shops (distribution), working from home

EXTENSION Ask students if they know of anyone who has set up a small business of this sort, and how it went.

Exercise 4

Students check the words they wrote down or heard from others in the class, and compare these with the kind of person they think Katia is.

Exercise 5

Students match the pairs of words with the appropriate definition.

Answers
1 characteristic b
  tendency a
2 grit b
  risk a
3 equity a
  debt b
4 grant a
  crowdfunding b
5 loan b
  lone a
6 venture capitalists a
  angel investors b
7 inspiration b
  perspiration a

Check word stress on these items and the pronunciation of the more difficult words, e.g. *debt, venture*. Note that students may have come across *grit* meaning very small pieces of stone or sand; however, it has a different meaning in the context of this unit.

Exercise 6

▶ **02** Give students time to read the six topics, a–f. Students then watch the entire interview with Thomas Hellmann and put the topics in order. Note that although the video is long, students only need to order the topics at this stage.

Answers
a 2 **b** 5 **c** 1 **d** 3 **e** 6 **f** 4

EXTENSION To help students digest the video, and before they hear parts of it again, ask if they heard anything in particular while they were watching. You can simply collect a few points or ideas, with minimal comment. This will help students listen out for those when they watch again.

Exercise 7

▶ 03 Give students time to read the five questions, and then watch the first part of the interview again to answer them.

Answers

1 It is one of the lines of research that has proven to be slightly difficult and frustrating for the simple reason that you can't box entrepreneurs into something very small and specific.
2 Entrepreneurs come in all varieties – definitely all genders, definitely all ages, definitely all ethnicities, definitely all backgrounds.
3 Entrepreneurs are risk-tolerant, but they're not risk-seekers. In fact, they see themselves as reducing risk. The job of an entrepreneur is not to take risk but to manage risk. The willingness to deal with risk is something that entrepreneurs need.
4 Controlling a situation and optimism are characteristics of entrepreneurs.
5 It's harder work and longer hours.

EXTENSION Ask which piece(s) of information they found most interesting, and why. They could also compare this to their own experiences, or people they know.

Exercise 8

Ask students to work with a partner and discuss the words. Which words describe them? Does their partner agree? Why/Why not? Open up the discussion and elicit answers from students as to whether or not they think they would make good entrepreneurs, and why.

PRE-WORK LEARNERS Students who have not yet started a career might be especially interested in discussing these words, and deciding if they themselves could be entrepreneurs.

PRONUNCIATION Help students with word stress on the two-part words, e.g. *risk-taker, hard-working, risk-seeker; risk-tolerant* can be stressed on either the first or second part.

Exercise 9

▶ 04 Students first read the list of possible sources of finance. They then watch the second part of the interview again and indicate the forms of financing he is positive and negative about, or doesn't comment on. Students can compare answers in pairs.

Answers

1 your bank manager ✗
2 debt ✗
3 equity ✓
4 credit cards ✗
5 loans or grants ✓
6 venture capitalists ✗
7 angel investors ?
8 crowdfunding ✓
9 family and friends ?

Draw students' attention to the *Glossary* of phrases used in the video.

Exercise 10

Students read the questions. Discuss them with the whole class.

ALTERNATIVE With a weaker group, it might be a good idea to let students make notes and work alone first, and then with a partner, before opening up the discussion to the whole class.

Exercise 11

▶ 05, 06 Students watch the last two parts of the interview and make notes in the table on reasons for failure and success.

ALTERNATIVE With a stronger group, you could ask students to guess or remember any reasons for failure and success first, before playing the last parts of the interview.

Answers

Two reasons for failure
1 failure of the initial idea but it leads to something else
2 failure after a longer period of time and you have to close the business

Three reasons for success
1 when your business is a personal passion
2 when entrepreneurs work in teams
3 when entrepreneurs have grit and work long hours

Exercise 12

Write the topic of the presentation on the board. Give students a few moments to think about it and what they could include. They could then share any ideas they have of their own, or from the video, and decide which are the most important and what order they would come in.

Draw students' attention to the three-part structure. They could use this to make notes against, and help organize the content of their talk.

ALTERNATIVE If students prefer, they could work in pairs to prepare and give their presentations.

Exercise 13

Students each give their presentations in turn. Encourage listeners to ask questions for clarification, or for presenters to expand on any points. Give credit for content (their ideas and the procedure), as well as language and organization.

Further ideas and video scripts

You can find a list of suggested ideas for how to use video in the class in the teacher resources in the *Online practice*. The video scripts are available to download from the Teaching resources on the Oxford Teachers' Club. www.oup.com/elt/teacher/businessresult

Unit content

By the end of this unit, students will be able to
- talk about technology
- deal with information and problems on the phone
- use phrasal verbs in different contexts.

Context

The topic of *Communications* refers both to the technology of communication and the importance of person-to-person communication in business.

The technology of communication has probably had the greatest impact both on the way business is done and what type of businesses have emerged. Firstly, it's hard to imagine our world without a mobile phone or Internet-based communication. Secondly, the boom in companies offering communications-related products seems unstoppable.

Most of your students will have noted the changes that communication technologies have brought to their working lives. It means the learning of new procedures and the need to be able to explain their complexities. It presents a new way of communicating with people in other countries and it has also opened doors to online conferences and online learning.

While some people still feel reluctant to engage fully with digital technology, others – especially the younger generation – are taking it for granted. Almost everyone communicates now by mobile phone, often using synced devices (e.g. with information updating automatically on their computer, smartphone and tablet) to carry out numerous everyday tasks. Increasingly also, mobile phones have enabled developing countries to leapfrog landlines and have played a significant role in the economic growth of these countries. The future stage will be machines communicating with machines and making decisions.

In this unit, students consider and discuss the impact of technology on communications, and the implications for business and organizations. Students are also encouraged to consider what aids better communication within groups or teams of people. *Business communication* and *Practically speaking* allow students to practise the language for dealing with information and resolving difficulties on the phone. In the *Talking point*, students work through a board game to practise different phone conversations.

Starting point

Students can discuss these questions as a class. Some issues which may come up are that communication technologies have improved our lives and given people the chance to keep in contact wherever they are in the world; but on the other hand, for many people, it has meant they are never out of contact, e.g. from their place of work. With regard to question 2, the majority of your students will probably rank their phone highly as a piece of technology they cannot live without.

Working with words

Exercise 1

Students look at the chart about online and digital tools and their usefulness in the workplace. They should consider how similar or different the results might be for themselves.

PRE-WORK LEARNERS Ask students to consider their own use of online and digital tools at their school or college and compare it to the chart.

Exercise 2

▶ **10.1** Students read the four questions and then listen to the report on the survey in **1** to answer them.

Answers
1 94%
2 Email is still used more than social media and texting, despite predictions.
3 Distractions were not increased. In fact, '46% of workers felt more productive and only 7% felt that their productivity had fallen.'
4 Company attitudes are less controlling towards Internet use. Less than 50% said their bosses put limits on usage, which is lower than in the past.

Exercise 3

▶ **10.1** Students complete the questions. They then listen again to check.

Answers
1 integrate, into
2 impact on
3 access to
4 focuses on
5 collaborate with
6 policy on
7 limits on
8 bring about

Exercise 4

Students take turns to ask and answer the questions in **3**. At the end, ask each pair to report back on their answers to two of the questions.

PRE-WORK LEARNERS Ask students to use the following revised questions to ask and answer with a partner.

1 How much do you need to integrate the Internet and mobile technology into your studies?

2 In what ways does digital technology impact on your daily life (at home, at college)?

3 For your studies, are there specific times when you are expected to have access to the Internet in order to liaise with other students, even when you are not at college?

4 The survey focuses on adult Internet users at work. Do you think the results in the chart would be similar for people's home life?

5 Do you often use video communication tools such as Skype to collaborate with students or friends in other parts of the world, for social or study reasons?

6 What is your college's policy on personal use of the Internet while you are at college?

7 Does your college put any limits on what students can say or post online? Does the college have guidelines or a policy on online posting?

8 What other changes do you think the Internet will bring about in the future?

Exercise 5

Suggest that students first skim the two texts to understand the general meaning. You could ask them the following questions:

Mercy Ships: *What are Mercy Ships?* (charity hospitals) *What is the connection between people working on the ship, and people working on land, miles away?* (doctors in real hospitals help volunteers on board the ship by controlling the equipment on the ship)

Mobile Entrepreneurs: *In what two areas are mobile phones helping business?* (paying for goods; delivering goods)

Then ask students to read the five missing sentences a–e, and add them to the text. Students can check their answers with a partner.

Answers
1 c 2 e 3 d 4 a 5 b

EXTENSION Ask students if they can think of other ways in which technology helps, or could help, people in developing countries.

Exercise 6

Students read the texts again. Check any difficult vocabulary before they answer the questions, e.g. *microscope, tissue samples, infrastructure*.

Answers
1 it allows doctors to work remotely
2 due to the lack of infrastructure

Exercise 7

Students build the words and complete the table.

DICTIONARY SKILLS
Students will find it helpful to refer to dictionaries for checking their answers to **7**. Also encourage them to check which syllable is stressed in each word.

Answers

Verb	Noun (person)	Noun	Adjective
	tech<u>ni</u>cian	tech<u>no</u>logy	<u>tech</u>nical/techno<u>lo</u>gical
<u>a</u>nalyse	<u>a</u>nalyst	a<u>na</u>lysis	ana<u>ly</u>tical/<u>a</u>nalysed
con<u>sult</u>	con<u>sult</u>ant	consul<u>ta</u>tion	con<u>sul</u>tative
de<u>ve</u>lop	de<u>ve</u>loper	de<u>ve</u>lopment	develop<u>men</u>tal/de<u>ve</u>loping
<u>in</u>novate	<u>in</u>novator	inno<u>va</u>tion	<u>in</u>novative
com<u>mu</u>nicate	com<u>mu</u>nicator	communi<u>ca</u>tion	com<u>mu</u>nicative
con<u>nect</u>		con<u>nec</u>tion	con<u>nec</u>ted
<u>transfer</u>		<u>transfer</u>	trans<u>fe</u>rable
e<u>co</u>nomize	e<u>co</u>nomist	e<u>co</u>nomy	eco<u>no</u>mical

EXTRA ACTIVITY
Ask students to underline the suffixes in columns 2–4 of the table. This will help them to notice the common endings for each type of word form. For example:

Noun (person): *-ian, -st, -ant, -er, - or, -ist*
Noun: *-ology, -is, -(at)ion, -ment, -er, -y*
Adjective: *-(ic)al, -ed, -ive, -ing, -able*

Further practice

If students need more practice, go to *Practice file 10* on page 124 of the *Student's Book*.

Exercise 8

You could begin by brainstorming and writing on the board all the types of communications technology students can think of. This will provide a useful springboard for the groups to discuss what has changed.

Listen for accuracy in students' use of vocabulary and the words in different forms.

PRE-WORK LEARNERS Students can discuss the changes that communications technology has brought about in life in general, such as in the home and in entertainment.

Exercise 9

Students use their notes from **8** to present their views to the class, giving examples from their own experience.

Photocopiable worksheet

Download and photocopy *Unit 10 Working with words* worksheet from the teacher resources in the *Online practice*.

Business communication

Exercise 1

Students read the questions and discuss them with a partner.

PRE-WORK LEARNERS Ask students to discuss their preferences for communicating with different groups of people, e.g. staff/tutors, friends, family, people they don't know. Ask why they use each medium in each case.

EXTENSION You could ask these further *questions*.
Do you feel you have to react more quickly to external clients' requests?
Do you take colleagues less seriously?

Also ask students how they think their language might change when dealing with colleagues and clients. With colleagues, the language is likely to be less formal but should still be helpful and service-orientated.

Exercise 2

▶ **10.2** Allow time for students to read the *Context* and the forms. JC Office Supplies works across Europe, but it has different centralized departments in different countries. Ask them which forms are for colleagues (1 and 2). To help with the listening, discuss what type of words students think they need to listen for. For example, gap 1 requires students to listen out for the name of a department, such as Human Resources or Production.

Answers
1 Sales
2 training course
3 02/584
4 check the figures and ask Angela to sign; fax contract to Training Direct.
5 blank screen but hard drive light is on
6 Look into the problem and call Johann back.
7 AS Consulting
8 order arrived out of office hours and left outside building / too much paper and no envelopes
9 check details and call back

Exercise 3

▶ **10.2** First, ask students to read the list of expressions, a–r. They then listen again and decide which conversation each was used in. They will probably need to listen twice while writing. Afterwards, they can compare their answers with the *Key expressions*.

Answers
b 2 **c** 3 **d** 1 **e** 2 **f** 1 **g** 2 **h** 1 **i** 2 **j** 1 **k** 3
l 2 **m** 1 **n** 1 **o** 2 **p** 1 **q** 3 **r** 1

Another way to focus students on phrases from the listening is to ask them to read the *Key expressions*. Then, as they listen, they number the phrases in the order they hear them used in the three conversations, or write the number of the conversation where the phrase is used.

Point out that many of these expressions include 'chunks' with a fixed meaning. Encourage your students to learn these as whole expressions, focusing on sentence stress and any linking sounds, e.g. *Talk me through it = Talk me through* /w/ *it. As_soon_as I've looked into it, …*

Note that the *Language point* in *Language at work* looks at some of these verbs within the context of phrasal verbs.

ALTERNATIVE To help students with the phrases, ask them to work with a partner. In turn, they say one key word as a prompt for their partner to give the full expression, e.g.
Student 1: *do*
Student 2: *What can I do for you today?*
Student 2: *straight*
Student 1: *Let me get this straight.*
etc.

Refer students to the *Tip*, and to the use of *by* and *until* when referring to deadlines. To help differentiate, it might help to explain that *until* relates to the whole period, which could be viewed as time 'horizontal', while *by* is the deadline, which may be seen as a vertical one-off point.

Further practice

If students need more practice, go to *Practice file 10* on page 124 of the *Student's Book*.

Exercise 4

Students work in pairs and role-play two different situations. Allocate A and B students and focus them on the information they need to read. Allow them time to read the situations and prepare what they will say, and remind them to think about which phrases from the *Key expressions* will be useful. Arrange students so they sit looking away from each other, in order to simulate a phone call and the lack of face-to-face contact.

Exercise 5

This exercise provides further practice with the language, but the task is much freer and requires students to create more of their own information.

You will obviously need to give feedback on use of the phrases from this section in the role-plays in both **4** and **5**. However, also focus on how helpful or polite each person sounded when serving the customer. Note that, even at this level, you may need to give remedial help with some of the language for giving details on times, dates, spellings or numbers. For example, the pronunciation of numbers, e.g. the /θ/ in *twentieth* or *fifth*, as well as differentiating word stress between *fifty* and *fifteen* can cause difficulties. Explaining locations or giving directions can also give even upper-intermediate students some problems.

Photocopiable worksheet

Download and photocopy *Unit 10 Business communication* worksheet from the teacher resources in the *Online practice*.

Practically speaking

Exercise 1

Students read the three situations and discuss with a partner what they would say in each one. Elicit some ideas.

Exercise 2

▶ 10.3 Students read the questions and then listen for the answers.

Exercise 3

▶ 10.3 Students match the statements and responses before listening again to check.

Answers
1 b 2 d 3 c 4 a

EXTENSION Ask students to look again at the phrases and decide which two are most familiar: what aspects would they change in each pair of phrases, e.g.
Sorry, but this'll have to be quick, I'm about to board a plane.
So now's not a good time to call?
I'm about to … go into a meeting / lecture / seminar; leave work/college; catch a bus, etc.
Then in pairs, and in turn, ask students to say one of their opening statements, and their partner to respond with a suitable reply.

Exercise 4

Students decide which statements in **3** indicate there is a problem in communication, and which indicate it isn't a good time to call.

Answers
problem in communication: 2, 3
not a good time to call: 1, 4

Exercise 5

For each situation, students need to be clear that there will be a problem with communication or that it isn't a good time to call. Talk through the situations and elicit some of the phrases which will be helpful. For example:
1 The person answering is on holiday so might say it's a bad time to call.
2 The line might be bad because the call is from a remote place.
3 The person is in the middle of watching a film and the phone call will disturb other viewers.
4 There will be a lot of noise from the sporting event so it will be difficult to hear.

Language at work

Exercise 1

Students underline the phrasal verbs in the eight sentences.

Answers
2	read back	6	hang up
3	look through	7	look into
4	put off	8	bring about
5	breaking up		

Exercise 2

Students now match the phrasal verbs to their meanings.

Answers
a	hang up	e	look through
b	bring about	f	call back
c	read back	g	look into
d	break up	h	put off

PRONUNCIATION Point out that the stress in phrasal verbs is on the particle, not on the verb, e.g. *OK, let me check that number. Could you read it back to me?*

Exercise 3

Students read the *Language point* and decide which verbs belong to each category. Encourage them to check the phrasal verbs in context in **1**. You could find the phrasal verbs for A together first.

You might like to point out that phrasal verbs in category A are sometimes referred to as 'intransitive', because they have no object. In addition, those in category B are sometimes called 'separable', and those in C 'inseparable', referring to whether we can separate the verb and the particle.

An example phrasal verb for category D is the following:
We decided to put the meeting off, or *We decided to put off the meeting*. But we can only say, *We decided to put it off*.

Answers
A breaking up, hang up
B look through (something), look into (something), bring about (something)
C read (something) back, call (someone) back
D put (something) off / put off (something)

DICTIONARY WORK
Encourage students to look the phrasal verbs up in a dictionary to find more example sentences. These will help them decide which category the phrasal verbs belong to.

Grammar reference

If students need more information, go to *Grammar reference* on page 125 of the *Student's Book*.

Exercise 4

Students work in pairs to make sentences from the phrasal verbs. Remind them to refer back to the *Language point* and to check word order.

Then ask them to match each sentence with one of the four categories, A–D, in the *Language point*.

Possible answers
We often eat out at this restaurant. = Category A
Look out! That box is about to fall on your head. = Category A
I'm putting Michael through now. = Category C
I'm looking for my pen. = Category B
He came across the idea in the laboratory. = Category B
Please write this message down. / Please write down this message. = Category D
Can you speak up? = Category A

ALTERNATIVE You could ask students to write a sentence for each phrasal verb and then swap their sentences with another pair. They then categorize each other's sentences.

Exercise 5

Students put the words in each sentence in the correct order. Do the first one together. Remind them that four sentences have two possible answers.

Answers
2 The project fell behind schedule.
3 He didn't carry out my instructions. / He didn't carry my instructions out.
4 You should take up their challenge. / You should take their challenge up.
5 Can you deal with this problem?
6 Let's weigh up the pros and cons.
7 The consultants drew it up.
8 I'd like to turn to the next point.
9 We need to speed up the team. / We need to speed the team up.
10 When did the entrepreneurs set up the company? / When did the entrepreneurs set the company up?

Further practice
If students need more practice, go to *Practice file 10* on page 125 of the *Student's Book*.

Exercise 6

Students work alone to write a short email using four or five phrasal verbs.

PRE-WORK LEARNERS Suggest students write an email either to one of their tutors or to one of their peers.

Exercise 7

Students swap their email with a partner and reply to the one they receive, again using some of the phrasal verbs. You could monitor as they do this. Make sure they also start and finish the emails appropriately!

You could collect the emails and check their use of phrasal verbs, and especially word order, after class. Alternatively, if the students agree, you could encourage peer correction: pass each pair of emails (two emails with two replies) to another pair of students. They should look specifically at the phrasal verbs and check they have been used correctly. Suggest they refer to the *Language point*. They could query anything they want to correct in pencil, or with a pencil question mark. They then pass the emails back to the original pair to be checked.

Photocopiable worksheet
Download and photocopy *Unit 10 Language at work* worksheet from the teacher resources in the *Online practice*.

Talking point

This *Talking point* is a game for students to practise a range of communicative language, including many of the phrases and vocabulary items from this unit, through a range of mini role-plays.

The aim of the game is to be the first to get from the Start square to the End square. Students can play in pairs or small groups. They will need a counter each (e.g. a ring), and one coin per group.

There is a range of coloured squares, each one with an instruction on it. Ask students to read the instructions at the top of the page so that they are aware of the different options they will have, or will be asked to do. To help them, you could look at one of each of the four different types of squares and elicit an answer for each one.

As the students play, listen in to different groups' games. Focus on effective communication (using the most appropriate phrase in a particular situation and using appropriate intonation to sound polite), as well as accuracy (meaning and word order).

When they have finished, find out who reached the end first, and also perhaps how many situations they had to role-play.

You could also ask them which squares included the easiest or most difficult situations and use this for revision.

ALTERNATIVE You could put on individual slips of paper, or on a list, all the vocabulary and phrases from this unit, i.e. the verbs from *Working with words*, the *Key expressions* from *Business communication* and the phrasal verbs from *Language at work*. Each group of students should try to use as many of the words and phrases together as possible, as they move through the game.

ONE-TO-ONE Play the game according to the rules, but have each phone conversation with each other. You could, however, include or each choose to play different roles, e.g. colleague, boss, client, etc., as appropriate.

Progress test
Download and photocopy *Unit 10 Progress test* and *Speaking test* from the teacher resources in the *Online practice*.

Unit content

By the end of this unit, students will be able to
- talk about change
- present plans and give balanced arguments
- talk about the probability of future activities and developments.

Context

The importance of *Change* in business is symbolized by the fact that we have the concept of 'change management', and 'change managers' who help organizations cope with change. You can even take courses in handling change.

Change affects us all, but it has become a key factor in business because companies recognize that once they have become successful, they must be prepared to change to remain competitive. In addition, the digital age has forced change at a much faster pace. Companies who do not keep up will suffer.

Once a business recognizes the need for change, there is the question of how to implement it. Classic mistakes include things being decided by upper management with little regard to how the rest of the workforce may react. Worse still is when change comes in the form of a faceless memo, sent to all departments, demanding change but with no suggestion of how to bring it about or how it will be supported over time. Without real support from staff and good management of new systems, change will not occur. In fact, change which is implemented badly may cause even more damage or ill-feeling than if things had been left unchanged.

In this unit, students consider the challenge of change for organizations and staff reactions to change. Most of your students will have experience of what it's like to cope with new systems and processes, either as the person trying to introduce change or the employee trying to cope with it. *Business communication* and *Language at work* help students to present and talk about future plans and changes. In the *Talking point*, students read about and discuss ways of implementing behavioural changes using the fun theory.

Starting point

Students can discuss the questions in small groups before sharing ideas with the class. Encourage students to give details and reasons for their answers.

PRE-WORK LEARNERS If students don't work for a company or don't think they have much experience of dealing with change at work, suggest they consider changes at college, at home, or in their way of life.

Working with words

Exercise 1

Students read the question and share their ideas with a partner.

Possible answers
Employees can react against a change; the change isn't sustained; the changes don't bring about a positive effect.

Exercise 2

▶ 11.1 Students listen to the presentation and write down what each of the five letters represents.

Answers
Awareness
Desire
Knowledge
Ability
Reinforcement

ALTERNATIVE Before listening, ask students to try to guess what the letters represent, based on their experience of change.

Exercise 3

▶ 11.1 Students first read the explanations and match them to the five steps. They then listen again to check.

Answers
1 desire
2 reinforcement
3 awareness
4 ability
5 knowledge

Exercise 4

Students read the questions and discuss their answers with a partner. Encourage them to give reasons for their answers.

PRE-WORK LEARNERS Ask students to consider if and how the ADKAR model could work in their school or college, e.g. to introduce a new course, or change how a course is run. Students can come up with other ideas of aspects which could be changed.
Then ask them to consider which of the five ADKAR steps would be most challenging, and why.

Exercise 5

Students read the pairs of words and then match them to definitions a or b.

Answers
1 op<u>pose</u> b / re<u>act</u> a
2 re<u>sist</u> a / pre<u>vent</u> b
3 <u>imp</u>lement b / re<u>vert</u> a
4 main<u>tain</u> a / sup<u>port</u> b
5 a<u>chieve</u> b / af<u>fect</u> a

PRONUNCIATION Ask students to underline the syllable which is stressed in each word (see Answers above).

EXTENSION Ask students if they are able to use any of the words in **5** to talk about situations in their own place of work or study, e.g. *At our company, they introduced a new system of weekly meetings; some people reacted because the times didn't suit and they had to change their routines.*

Exercise 6

Students complete the missing words 1–8 in the article. Suggest they do this first without referring back to the words in **5**.

Answers
1 implement
2 affect
3 react
4 accept
5 oppose
6 support
7 resist
8 prevent

DICTIONARY SKILLS

Ask students to use their dictionaries to find the noun form of each verb in **5**: check that they notice any spelling changes, e.g. *maintain → main**ten**ance*. They should also check the word stress; in some cases, the stress shifts, e.g. *op<u>pose</u> → oppo<u>si</u>tion*.

Answers
oppo<u>si</u>tion, re<u>ac</u>tion, re<u>sis</u>tance, pre<u>ven</u>tion, implemen<u>ta</u>tion, re<u>ver</u>sion, <u>main</u>tenance, sup<u>port</u>, a<u>chieve</u>ment, affec<u>ta</u>tion

Draw students' attention to the difference in meaning between the verbs *effect* – to make something happen, and *affect* – to produce a change in someone or something. Point out that *effect* can be both a verb and a noun.

Exercise 7

Students categorize the words from the article in **6**. Encourage them to read the article again to help.

Answers
1 *concerned*, anxious
2 hostile, criticism, resistance, ambivalent
3 in favour of, receptive, guidance, optimism, enthusiasm

Further practice
If students need more practice, go to *Practice file 11* on page 126 of the *Student's Book*.

Exercise 8

Ask students to read the first question and to share their choice and reasons with a partner. Where possible, ask them to support their choice with examples or evidence.

Then ask them to consider point 2 together. Elicit some of their ideas.

ALTERNATIVE You could ask students to tick off the words in **5** and **7** as they use them.

Exercise 9

Students work in small groups. They should choose one of the changes. They then follow the ADKAR model, answer the questions and discuss how they would implement the change.

PRE-WORK LEARNERS Students could consider one of the listed changes in relation to their place of study; alternatively, they could choose one of the following:
– moving some of the face-to-face classes online (with, for example, a dedicated learning platform, a forum for discussions, etc.)
– changing the times/days of (some of) the classes
– handing over more control to participants (e.g. in terms of curriculum design, lesson organization, assignment choice, etc.).

ONE-TO-ONE Together you could choose one of the changes and work through the ADKAR model; alternatively, you could choose one change each, and then share the ideas you have for implementing it according to the ADKAR model and offer improvements.

Photocopiable worksheet
Download and photocopy *Unit 11 Working with words* worksheet from the teacher resources in the *Online practice*.

Business communication

Exercise 1

This discussion acts as a lead-in to the section.

Note that students' answers to these questions will depend on the culture of their company and their country. In some cultures, it is the norm that management makes all decisions and employees have little opportunity to comment. If you are teaching a group from a company, it is possible that some of your students may feel quite critical of the company's current decision-making processes. Be aware that these issues may need to be handled sensitively.

PRE-WORK LEARNERS Students could consider how (educational) decisions affecting them are made in their college: Are they consulted about changes? If so, how? (e.g. in writing, online, in a meeting, etc.) Are they encouraged to make suggestions for any changes or improvements?

Exercise 2

▶ 11.2 Tell students they are going to listen to a presentation by Rachel and Imran. Ask them to read the *Context* and find out what the presentation is about and who these people are. (The presentation is about proposed changes suggested by business consultants to make FGR more efficient. Rachel and Imran are department leaders.) Check students understand the *Context* (i.e. what the presentation is about, and who the people are). Students then listen and complete the notes.

Answers
1 through 'natural wastage'*
2 through departmental meetings and updates on the Intranet
3 by the end of the month
4 Most employees are free on Friday afternoons and the forum will mean staying at work longer.
5 Yes, if management sees real results after the changes are made.
*natural wastage = reducing the workforce by not replacing employees who leave through retirement or resignation

Exercise 3

▶ 11.2 Students match 1–10 to a–j to make expressions and then listen again to check.

Answers
1 c 2 g 3 h 4 a 5 i 6 b 7 f 8 d 9 e 10 j

Exercise 4

Students turn to audio script 11.2 on page 150 of the *Student's Book* and identify the phrases for 1 and 2.

Note that in the presentation, Imran uses the phrase *Let's digress for a moment* … . Refer students to the *Tip* for more on this use of *Let's*.

Answers
1 I'd like to pass the next point over to …
2 Let's digress for a moment and look at this in more detail …

Further practice

If students need more practice, go to *Practice file 11* on page 126 of the *Student's Book*.

Exercise 5

Before students work in pairs, allow them a few minutes to find suitable phrases from the *Key expressions* and think of how to structure their sentences. Some students may want to write the sentences first. This is fine as long as you ask them to cover them up when speaking with their partner.

Exercise 6

Students read the list of topics and choose one that relates to their job. Alternatively, they can make up a new situation entirely.

PRE-WORK LEARNERS Students could consider their college syllabus or, for example, assignments and/or how they are assessed.

Exercise 7

Students work in pairs and give their presentation to their partner, who listens and ticks off any phrases they hear from the *Key expressions*.

ALTERNATIVE Students could work in pairs on the same presentation with each of them giving half of it. Remind them to use the phrase *I'd like to pass the next point over to …* halfway through in order to let their partner carry on.

During the presentations, the students listening tick the phrases used and could ask questions at the end about the changes.

ALTERNATIVE Ask students to work in groups of three to give their presentation. While they do this, one person gives the presentation, one ticks off the phrases they hear and the third person listens to the content and prepares two or three questions to ask at the end.

While students listen and tick phrases, ask them also to listen out for any phrases which are incorrect. Encourage peer feedback afterwards.

EXTRA ACTIVITY
Put students into groups of four. One student gives their presentation from **7**. The listening students are all given a role from the article in *Working with words* on page 73 (supporter, ambivalent, opponent). The presenter speaks and then takes questions and reactions at the end. The listening students play their roles and react accordingly. After five minutes, stop the activity and everyone changes roles so there is a new presenter and each listener responds in a new way. By the end, everyone has presented and been a different kind of listener. The role-play will be fun but it also will let students see/feel what it's like to respond in different ways to change. Discuss students' reactions to the activity afterwards.

Photocopiable worksheet

Download and photocopy *Unit 11 Business communication* worksheet from the teacher resources in the *Online practice*.

Practically speaking

Exercise 1

Students read the question and share their ideas with a partner. Elicit some of their ideas.

PRE-WORK LEARNERS Students could consider discussions with peers or staff/tutors at their school or college, and why it's important to consider both sides of an argument. This could include discussions about assignment criteria, deadlines and evaluation, as well as in-class activities where students may be asked to openly discuss a topic with other students and present their opinion and rationale.

Possible answer
It is important to consider both sides of an argument so that you don't overlook anything.

Exercise 2

▶ **11.3** Students read the four headings and then make notes for and against, as they listen to the conversations.

Answers
1 **Changing the team meeting**
  For: Can never get everyone together in the same place at the same time during the week so it's the only option.
  Against: People on flexitime often choose to leave early on Fridays. / Everyone's concentration probably won't be as good at the end of the week.
2 **Restructuring**
  For: streamline the company's operation
  Against: a clever way of getting rid of staff; employees are naturally worried
3 **Learning Spanish**
  For: having a common language for the company
  Against: staff who aren't confident in their language skills might find it difficult
4 **Extending office hours**
  For: should improve the service
  Against: not certain that it will generate the extra revenue needed

Exercise 3

▶ **11.3** Students listen again and write down the phrases the speakers use to give both sides of the argument. You could suggest they do this in two columns, one FOR and one AGAINST.

Answers
1 I have some reservations about it, too. / But I can also see the point of moving it.
2 I can see both sides of the argument. / On the one hand … but on the other hand …
3 It sounds interesting – I like the idea of … / though I also understand that …
4 I'm not sure. The main argument for it is … / But the argument against it is …

EXTENSION Ask students to group the phrases into FOR, AGAINST and BOTH, and to try to add one or two more expressions, e.g. FOR: *I go along with that; This makes a lot of sense;* AGAINST: *I'm really not convinced (about …); I don't like the idea of …; I can't see the point of -ing/(noun) …;* BOTH: *While it's true that …, I don't think …*

Exercise 4

Students work in pairs. They should read the four proposals, and then discuss these and express both sides of the argument using the phrases from **3**.

PRE-WORK LEARNERS Students could discuss the topics listed, or one of the following:
– colleges / higher education to provide free drinking water and plastic cups in communal spaces
– colleges / higher education to loan bicycles to students to avoid having to use public transport or their own cars
– moving some of the classes to the evenings / Saturday mornings to make more space for other activities in the buildings
– making all lectures available on video for students to watch (a second time) in their free time

ALTERNATIVE If you have a small group (three or four students only), you could read out the proposals in turn. Ask one of the students to express their view; then ask the next student to comment on that opinion and then express a different opinion. Then the next does the same. This will help them listen, focus and present a more balanced argument.

Remind students that the skill of being able to see and comment on both sides of an argument is increasingly relevant nowadays. Being aware of these phrases will help them to listen more attentively and demonstrate respect when communicating with people with different opinions and views.

Language at work

Exercise 1

Students read the sentences and underline the future verb forms.

Answers
1 A final decision <u>will</u> definitely <u>have</u> <u>been</u> <u>reached</u> by March. (future perfect)
2 Over the next few weeks, we'<u>ll</u> <u>be</u> <u>hosting</u> departmental meetings. (future continuous)
3 I probably <u>won't</u> <u>be</u> <u>going</u> anywhere on that day. (future continuous)

Exercise 2

Students read the questions in the *Language point* and match the sentences from **1**.

Answers
a 2 **b** 3 **c** 1 **d** after *will* **e** before *won't*

PRONUNCIATION Remind students that, in speaking, the words *have* and *been* are often contracted, i.e. *will have been* /wɪləvbɪn/.

EXTENSION Ask students to think of three ideas of their own, perhaps true and in their diaries, which they can tell each other about using the three future tenses in **1**, e.g. *I will definitely have finished my project by August. / Over the next few weeks, I'll be spending more time learning English vocabulary. / I probably won't be at home on Saturday.*

Grammar reference
If students need more information, go to *Grammar reference* on page 127 of the *Student's Book*.

Exercise 3

The aim in this exercise is for students to produce sentences containing the future continuous and future perfect.

Possible answers
1 They'll be clearing the ground over the next six months.
  They'll be cutting down trees …
  They'll be taking on temporary workers …
2 They'll have completed the project by this time next year.
  They'll have built a new supermarket …
  They'll have created local jobs …

Exercise 4

▶ 11.4 Students listen to identify what is being discussed in each extract.

Answers
1 the end of a project
2 problems for the government – inflation and the economy
3 a speaker withdrawing from a conference

Exercise 5

This exercise helps students differentiate between degrees of probability. Students find the phrases in audio script 11.4 on page 150 of the *Student's Book* and write the percentages.

Answers
Extract 1: bound to 100%
            probably won't 25%
            there's a good chance 75%
Extract 2: it is doubtful 25%
            is certain to 100%
            are likely to 75%
Extract 3: definitely won't 0%
            'll probably 75%
            perhaps 50%
            will definitely 100%

Further practice
If students need more practice, go to *Practice file 11* on page 127 of the *Student's Book*.

Exercise 6

Students discuss 1 and 2, using the phrases in **5** and the correct tenses. You could suggest that they try to use a range of ways to express probability.

ALTERNATIVE Ask students to write down three sentences, based on the questions in **6**, using the correct tenses and phrases to express probability. Two of the sentences should be true, while one is false. They work in pairs, read out their sentences, and their partner has to guess which one is false by asking questions, e.g.:
Student A: *I'm bound to have finished the report by Friday.*
Student B: *Have you started yet? Is it easy to write? What is the deadline?*, etc.

Exercise 7

Students work in pairs and discuss possible developments in their industry or at their place of work. They could first brainstorm ideas on a piece of paper and then formulate them into full sentences.

PRE-WORK LEARNERS Students discuss their own area of study, or could discuss possible changes in the future in education based on technology.

Exercise 8

Pair students up with another pair. They should compare their predictions and comment on their likelihood.

Listen out for use of future tenses, as well as phrases for expression of probability, and give feedback on good use of these, as well as areas which need correcting.

Photocopiable worksheet
Download and photocopy *Unit 11 Language at work* worksheet from the teacher resources in the *Online practice*.

Talking point

Discussion

Exercise 1

Ask students to read the text and decide if they would change their behaviour as a result of the ideas mentioned in the article. Students compare their ideas with a partner. Elicit any which show how students might change their behaviour!

Exercise 2

Students read the two questions and discuss their ideas with a partner. Elicit a few ideas.

PRE-WORK LEARNERS Ask students to think of examples from their study or home context, or any work experience, where money has been effective in changing their or others' behaviour, e.g. a rebate (money back) on a course fee (or part of it) if they pass the final exams (encouraging them to study more); discounts on future purchases for recycling or returning used products (e.g. coffee capsules, empty bottles, etc.); not having to pay the weekly fee for a dieting/gym club if you've kept your weight down over the previous week.

Exercise 3

Students read the question. Ask them to share their ideas with a partner. Elicit their ideas, encouraging them to give reasons.

Task

Exercise 1

Students work in groups of three to come up with ideas to change employees' behaviour.

ALTERNATIVE Students work in three groups, each with one of the topics and an A4 sheet. Give them three minutes to come up with and write down any ideas they have. Moving from one sheet to the next, they will see each other's ideas, which may prompt them to come up with more ideas!

ONE-TO-ONE You could choose one topic together and write down each idea you have on a separate slip of paper. Try to use as many slips of paper as possible!

Exercise 2

Students in turn present their best idea(s) and give their explanations. Encourage other students to comment, or challenge, and to ask questions.

Exercise 3

Students think of another example of behaviour they would like to change and discuss how they could apply 'fun theory'.

> **EXTRA ACTIVITY**
> Students could discuss 'fun theory' with colleagues outside of class and come up with a real idea to implement.

Progress test
Download and photocopy *Unit 11 Progress test* and *Speaking test* from the teacher resources in the *Online practice*.

12 Data

Unit content

By the end of this unit, students will be able to
- talk about data
- describe trends
- report what someone has said.

Context

It is often said that people suffer from information overload in the twenty-first century and that the Internet is responsible for a great deal of this. Its ability to provide facts and figures at the click of a mouse has meant that we can find out virtually anything straight away. Consumers can research prices and specifications of products. Students use it for educational research. For others, access to facts and figures has simply become an addiction, with many people searching for 'trivia' or facts which do not necessarily have any relevance or importance in life, but are easy to come by and enjoyable.

Facts and figures are, however, relevant and necessary for people working in business. They present them, exchange them and interpret them. In this unit, students work with facts and figures in the context of the Internet. Of particular relevance these days is how much personal information we willingly put online, whether it is data through social media, or personal preferences when searching for and buying products online; companies are increasingly using this information to target users with specific information, advertising or products.

Business communication focuses on how advertising has evolved on the Internet. Students will have experience of this either as a consumer or as part of a company which is making use of the Internet. Talking about numbers and describing trends are also looked at.

In the *Talking point*, students look at 'statisticulation': how some people misuse statistics intentionally. Students then have the opportunity to look at some sample statistics and consider ways of checking these for statisticulation.

Starting point

Students read and discuss the questions with a partner. You could start by brainstorming one or two examples of data and/or information collection about customers, and ways of collecting it.

Possible answers
2 data/Information, e.g. contact information; age, gender, profession (demographics); personal tastes and preferences; payment preferences, etc.
How: website activity (traffic), social media use, in person, etc.

Note that issues relating to privacy will come up in the reading text which follows.

PRE-WORK LEARNERS Ask students to consider what information their college or place of study has on them. What other information would be useful for the college? What ways are there to collect this information? They could think about potential and current students.

Working with words

Exercise 1

Students read and discuss the questions. This time they are looking at information from the perspective of the customer (not the company). Give students two or three minutes and then elicit some of their ideas.

Exercise 2

Students read the text quickly and match the headings 1–3 with the paragraphs, A–C.

Answers
1 C 2 A 3 B

Exercise 3

Students read the questions and then read the text again to find the answers. Check students understand *obsessed* (line 1), and *make sense (of something)* (line 3). They can discuss their ideas with a partner.

Answers
1 no, only that it is a challenge to make sense of it all
2 Amazon uses information on past purchases, EE on customer behaviour and Starbucks on traffic flows and demographics when planning to open a new store.
3 Questionnaires and surveys still have a purpose for certain information, e.g. data such as age, profession, gender, and marital status.
4 through web activity, social media and with special software tracking mouse movements
5 Make sure your approach is legal.

Exercise 4

Students read the definitions and then find a word or words in the corresponding paragraph, A, B or C.

Answers

2	data analytics	**7**	data gathering
3	customer behaviour	**8**	cookies
4	demographics	**9**	privacy policy
5	data-driven	**10**	data breach
6	transactional history		

Exercise 5

Students work through questions 1–6 and add the missing words. Suggest they refer back to their answers in **4** to help.

Answers

1	analytics	**4**	transactional
2	driven	**5**	breach
3	demographics	**6**	privacy

Exercise 6

Students work in pairs to ask and answer the questions in **5**.

EXTRA ACTIVITY

Students work in small groups. Give each group one of the following nouns: *data, policy, customer*.
They should think of other nouns which they can combine with their word to make compound nouns (e.g. *data storage, insurance policy, customer care*), and write them on an A4 sheet. You could encourage them to check their ideas in a dictionary. Give them two or three minutes, and then ask them to pass their paper to another group. Students try to add any more combinations they know. Pass the papers on once more. Then ask students to try to use two noun combinations from each list to talk about a work issue, or something they have heard in the news.

Possible answers

data: ~ storage, ~ retrieval, ~ analysis, ~ management, ~ processing, ~ system, ~ capture, ~ stream, ~ collection

policy: ~ document, ~ statement, ~ decision, ~ making, insurance ~

customer: ~ care, ~ relations, ~ service, ~ support, ~ agreement, ~ satisfaction, ~ complaints

---

Exercise 7

Students match the verbs 1–9 with nouns a–i. They can check their answers in the article in **2**.

Answers

1 g   2 i   3 f   4 a   5 h   6 d   7 c   8 b   9 e

EXTRA ACTIVITY

Ask students to choose three verb + noun combinations from **7** which they would like to use. They should think of an example they know, or have experienced, for each one, e.g. *If you analyse data on Twitter, you can find out which tweets are most popular.* Or, *Using software to track the movements of a mouse on the screen would help monitor [the] behaviour of potential customers who visit our website.*

Further practice

If students need more practice, go to *Practice file 12* on page 128 of the *Student's Book*.

Exercise 8

Students work in small groups. They should read the two business proposals and make a list of data each company would need, and how they could collect it.

ALTERNATIVE If you have a small class, divide them into two groups and give one business proposal and an A4 sheet to each one. Give them a time limit to come up with data, and ways of collecting it. Then pair up the two groups, or ask each person to find a partner with someone from the other group, and to present their ideas.

ONE-TO-ONE You could each look at one of the proposals, and then discuss them both. Alternatively, you could discuss together each one in turn. Then, as a model, summarize your recommendations on one of the proposals and ask your student to do the same on the other proposal.

Exercise 9

Students join another group and present their ideas. At this point, they should be trying to use the vocabulary from **4**, **5** and **7**. The others should listen to their recommendations. Encourage them to ask questions for clarification.

Give credit for accurate use of noun combinations and elicit corrections for any they have difficulty with.

EXTENSION At the end, ask students to vote on the best recommendation for the type of data and/or how to collect it.

ALTERNATIVE Suggest that, as students tell each other about their recommendations, they get points for each word combination they use. You could ask one student from each group to record or tick these off.

Photocopiable worksheet

Download and photocopy *Unit 12 Working with words* worksheet from the teacher resources in the *Online practice*.

Business communication

Exercise 1

Discuss these questions as a class. Ask students to give examples of the most common types.

The listening in **2** includes some vocabulary which some students might want to know more about.

blogs = short for *web logs* which are web pages written by individuals either about their own lives or a topic or issue they are interested in. Some blogs attract many visitors.

podcasts = files (often audio) delivered to users via subscription (often free)

RSS feeds = files containing short amounts of information sent to users to encourage them to visit a much larger site, e.g. a news organization can send a user breaking news

user-generated media = media including blogs, podcasts and RSS feeds which are created by independent online users

In advertising terms, many companies have recognized that these kinds of media provide a much more direct and effective way to reach target audiences.

Exercise 2

▶ **12.1** When students have read the *Context*, ask: *Why would online advertising be particularly effective for SurAuto.com?* The answer is probably that it targets younger drivers who will often use the Internet.

Play the listening and students make notes on what the figures refer to.

> **Answers**
> 1 age of the target market
> 2 growth in advertising spending on blogs and podcasts
> 3 the proportion spent on blog advertising
> 4 the projected expenditure on blog advertising in four years
> 5 the annual compound growth rate of podcast advertising

Exercise 3

Students match the two halves of the phrases 1–10 to a–j.

Exercise 4

▶ **12.1** Students listen again and check their answers.

Draw students' attention to the *Key expressions*. You could ask them to underline the prepositions, as these are an important part of some of the phrases, e.g. *fill us in on …*; *according to …*; etc.

When checking answer 3, you can refer to the *Tip*. Note that using these words helps distance the speaker from the fact, or even an opinion. It may be useful to point out this sort of nuance to your students.

> **Answers**
> 1 e 2 c 3 i 4 a 5 g 6 d 7 h 8 j 9 b 10 f

> **EXTRA ACTIVITY**
> Ask students to choose five phrases from **3** which they would like to learn and use; this should include phrases which ask for factual or numerical information, as well as phrases which report or summarize findings. Note that it is the beginning of each phrase which is the most important (the rest of the phrase will change in their contexts). Then, in pairs, ask them to share the phrases they have chosen and reduce their joint list of ten phrases to a total of five, based on which phrases they both agree are the most useful or important. When they have done this, ask them to decide which one or two (maximum) key words they will 'keep' to remind them of the phrases. They should write each key word on a slip of paper, e.g.
> *Could you fill us in on the most relevant information from the seminar?* > key word: *fill* (or *fill in*)
> *Apparently, a recent study shows a huge increase in …* > key word: *apparently* (or *apparently/shows*)
> You could suggest students use their cue cards (slips of paper with key words on them) in **5**. For this next activity, students could work with a different partner.

Further practice

If students need more practice, go to *Practice file 12* on page 128 of the *Student's Book*.

Exercise 5

This is an information-gap activity where students have to report and ask for information on blog advertising. Students will practise saying figures and should also be trying to use the phrases from the section. Note that the Comments column in the table suggests conclusions and provides information to interpret the facts and figures given. Remind students to refer to the phrases in the *Key expressions*. At the end, students compare their tables to check the information is correct.

Monitor for use of the phrases, but also work on any individual problems with saying particular numbers.

Photocopiable worksheet

Download and photocopy *Unit 12 Business communication* worksheet from the teacher resources in the *Online practice*.

Practically speaking

Exercise 1

Ask students to read the three ways of dealing with advertising emails and to share their ideas with the class.

Ask students to discuss the second question with a partner and then elicit a few ideas to share with the class.

EXTENSION Ask students if they have any other strategies for dealing with advertising emails.

PRE-WORK LEARNERS Students will be able to answer the first question. For the second question, ask them about their own experiences of receiving emails which are obviously part of a marketing campaign. What sort of companies do the emails come from? What do the students do with the emails? How relevant are they to their life / work / studies? How useful do they think the campaigns are to the companies? Why?

Exercise 2

▶ **12.2** Students read the questions and then listen to the extract. You may need to play the listening twice. Students can check their answers with a partner.

> **Answers**
> 1 approximately 5,000
> 2 better (because of the click through)
> 3 the offer of a 20% discount

Exercise 3

▶ **12.2** Students listen again and match the phrases with the information they refer to.

> **Answers**
> 1 c 2 a 3 d 4 b

EXTENSION Ask students about their own experiences of 'clicks': for example, what is their own click rate for advertising emails? How often do they click through? They could also think about their behaviour online in relation to links on social media.

Exercise 4

Students add the phrases from **3** to the scale.

Exercise 5

Students add the other phrases to the scale, as well as any others they can think of (suggested answers in brackets below). Get them to compare their ideas before going over the answers.

Answers
fast/big fall: plummet, (significant drop)
slow/small fall: slight drop, (minor dip)
no change: remain steady, (stay the same)
slow/small rise: steady increase, (slight upturn)
fast/big rise: significant jump, (substantial hike)

Exercise 6

Students read the topics and then use phrases from **3** and **5** to talk about them.

Check they use the phrases accurately, and with the appropriate preposition, e.g. a *noticeable rise in …*; *compared to/with …*; *from … to …*, etc.

PRE-WORK LEARNERS Students could focus on the list of changes, or talk about one of the following: the number of students learning a foreign language in their circle of friends; prices of goods or services important and relevant to them (e.g. transport fares). If they are unsure of the information, they could guess (and perhaps check later).

ALTERNATIVE Give students small slips of paper and ask them to write down five expressions they'd like to use, one on each slip. They discuss the topics and place the slip on the table when they use that phrase.

> **EXTRA ACTIVITY**
> Students could do some mini-research out of class, and choose a topic to find out specific data about. It could be one of the topics listed in **6**, or another topic where they can use specific figures, and talk about recent changes and trends. They could then report their ideas back to the class next time.

Language at work

Exercise 1

Students read the questions and share their ideas with the class.

Exercise 2

Students read the questions and then read the text to find the answers. They can share their answers with a partner. Check the pronunciation of *vinyl* /ˈvaɪnl/.

Answers
1 a slow decline
2 the rapid growth in vinyl record sales; music streaming sites are boosting sales, vinyls for décor, nice to have an object you can hold and physically play, and supporting the artists

EXTENSION Ask students if they are surprised at any of the information in the text. Why? What do they think about vinyl records? Do they or would they like to own any? Do they know of any iconic album record sleeve covers?
You could also find out what they think about making sure artists are supported financially, and how this works on music streaming websites.

Exercise 3

Students underline the eight sentences which report what someone said. Find the first one together.

Answers
… it was reported that sales of vinyl albums have increased dramatically …

… a recent consumer survey concluded that music streaming sites are boosting this growth …

The survey also asked them how much they had listened to the record …

48% admitted that they hadn't played it …

… 7% said they didn't even own a turntable.

One student explained, 'I have vinyls in my room but it's more for décor. I don't actually play them'.

Another 18-year-old told a reporter that it was nice to have an object you could hold and physically play.

She added, 'I also think it's important to support artists financially if you can.'

Exercise 4

Students read and answer the questions in the *Language point*. They can share their answers with a partner.

Answers
1 **Direct speech:**
    One student explained, 'I have vinyls in my room but it's more for décor. I don't actually play them'.
    She added, 'I also think it's important to support artists financially if you can'.
    Reported speech:
    … it was reported that sales of vinyl albums have increased dramatically …
    … a recent consumer survey concluded that music streaming sites are boosting this growth …
    The survey also asked them how much they had listened to the record …
    48% admitted that they hadn't played it …
    … 7% said they didn't even own a turntable.
    Another 18-year-old told a reporter that it was nice to have an object you could hold and physically play.
2 reported, concluded, admitted, said, explained, told, added; asked (for questions)
3 subject–verb
4 a person
5 **a** The reported information is still true/happening at the time of reporting.
    b Because it was originally said using the present perfect.

Grammar reference
If students need more information, go to *Grammar reference* on page 129 of the *Student's Book*.

Exercise 5

Students complete the sentences using the verb in the appropriate tense.

Answers
1 had sold over six hundred thousand records in the first three months
2 are currently selling
3 in the USA, vinyl sales were worth $416 million
4 thought about the level of service from mobile phone companies
5 prefers watching videos online to watching TV
6 didn't/don't tell them about downloads among the over 50s

You could mention that, even if you change the tense of the reporting verb, it's still possible to use the present tense because the reported information is still true/relevant at the time of reporting, e.g. in 2 and 5:

2 He said that they are currently selling more than ever.

5 One person told us that she prefers watching videos online.

Further practice
If students need more practice, go to *Practice file 12* on page 129 of the *Student's Book*.

Exercise 6

Students first work on their own to recall a conversation with a customer or colleague. You could suggest they write it down, as a conversation, e.g:

Me: …

Colleague: …

They could also think about the reporting verbs they want to use. Remind them to check the *Language point*.

Then ask them to work with a partner and report the conversations to each other.

Feed back on accurate use of tenses, word order and the range of reporting verbs.

PRE-WORK LEARNERS Ask students to think of an important conversation they had with a peer or tutor/member of staff.

Photocopiable worksheet
Download and photocopy *Unit 12 Language at work* worksheet from the teacher resources in the *Online practice*.

Talking point

Discussion

Exercise 1

This section looks at how some people misuse statistics intentionally.

Check students are clear of the meaning of *statisticulation* (and can pronounce it!). Then ask students to read the question, and then read the text to find suitable questions they could ask. Ask them to share their ideas with a partner, before sharing them with the class.

Exercise 2

Students read the questions and share their ideas. Draw attention to the two graphs, and how the data can be made to look different. You could elicit one or two first, e.g. a survey in which most people who responded were female, or one where patients at a surgery were asked about their willingness to visit a doctor (which excludes those who are at home because they don't want to).

Exercise 3

Discuss the questions as a class. Find out what information and data would be used by the students' companies and how it is presented to customers and clients.

PRE-WORK LEARNERS Ask students to think about data and information that would be important to their school or college, e.g. where students come from, what results they get in exams, etc., and how this information could be presented in a variety of ways and interpreted differently.

Task

Exercise 1

Ask the students to read the four sets of statistics. For each one, they should think of questions they could ask to check the facts and date, and whether any of it has been misused.

ALTERNATIVE You could ask students first to underline the key information in each set of statistics, and think of how each item could be checked or proved, e.g. *research participants* (how many, what age, where from, what backgrounds, etc.), and so on.

ALTERNATIVE If you have a large group, you could ask each group to look at just one set of statistics and then share their ideas with the class.

ONE-TO-ONE You could work together on one set of statistics, and then choose one more each to work on, and then share and discuss your ideas afterwards.

Exercise 2

Students consider how each statistic could influence how a company works with its staff or customers. Encourage participants to come up with more than one idea.

Possible answers
Companies might decide to redesign offices, and use open-plan space; or they may include low-level background music. Companies may change illustrations used on advertising, or product packaging, in order to appeal to right-handed people. If companies have an in-house canteen or café/restaurant, companies might decide to redesign the use of space to have fewer but larger tables to accommodate more people. Companies may consider other ways to make customers feel 'special' or especially chosen.

ALTERNATIVE You could do this with the whole class, or ask students to work in pairs or small groups.

Progress test
Download and photocopy *Unit 12 Progress test* and *Speaking test* from the teacher resources in the *Online practice*.

Viewpoint 4

Preview

The topic of this *Viewpoint* is *Social media marketing*. Students begin by discussing traditional forms of advertising, and the advantages and disadvantages of these. They then watch an interview in four parts with one of the world's leading academic marketing experts (much of the information is based on social media marketing). Students hear about which products benefit from this sort of marketing, and how it works. Finally, they do a task which involves planning their own digital media strategy, considering ways in which they can make both traditional and social media marketing work well together.

Exercise 1

Give time for students to consider the traditional forms of advertising and read the example. Then ask them to form small groups to think of another advantage and disadvantage for each.

ALTERNATIVE You could ask students to think of a specific advert for each form of traditional advertising. This will help them evaluate its advantages and disadvantages.

Exercise 2

Ask students to form new groups to share their ideas, and to note down any other advantages or disadvantages they hear. Then discuss the ideas as a class.

Possible answers

Type of advertising	Advantages	Disadvantages
Newspaper or magazine	You can target the type of people who buy a particular type of newspaper or magazine.	Lots of people ignore the adverts in these types of media.
Posters, leaflets and billboards	Cheap and has visual impact.	Lots of people throw leaflets away or drive past billboards without looking at them.
Television	Reaches a large number of people and you can target viewers according to programmes.	Very expensive. People often do something else when the adverts are on, e.g. make a cup of tea.
Radio	Reaches a wide audience. Cheap to make.	Lacks visual impact. Hard to target a type of customer.

Exercise 3

Refer students to the *Profile* of Professor Andrew Stephen. Then ask them to read the words and phrases 1–12 and match them to the definitions a–l. As you check their answers, check students' pronunciation, especially of the following: *utilitarian; hedonic; dissemination; synergistically* /ˌsɪnəˈdʒɪstɪkli/; *silos*.

Answers
1 h 2 a 3 e 4 d 5 g 6 f 7 l 8 j 9 k 10 b
11 c 12 i

Exercise 4

▶ **01** Before playing the video, give students time to read the words and phrases 1–9. Then, as they watch the first part of the interview with Professor Andrew Stephen, students decide whether the words relate to traditional (T) or social media (S) advertising. Do not check answers now, as they will compare answers in **5** and then check.

ALTERNATIVE You could give time for students to make guesses about whether the words and phrases refer to traditional or social media advertising before playing the video.

Exercise 5

▶ **01** Students work in pairs to explain their answers in **4**. Then play the video again for them to check and confirm.

Answers
1 T 2 T 3 S 4 S 5 S 6 S 7 T 8 T 9 S

Exercise 6

▶ **02** Draw students' attention to the table and ask them to make notes according to types of products, and how social media works. Then play the video. Do not check answers now, as they will compare answers in **7** and then add any missing information.

Exercise 7

▶ 02 Students compare their answers in pairs. Then play the video again and encourage them to add to their notes.

Suggested answers

Types of products social media advertises …	How social media can work …
more effectively: high consideration goods, utilitarian items such as insurance	more effectively: when it doesn't come across as an ad, but is more like a conversation or feels personal
less effectively: hedonic goods such as movie tickets	less effectively: when it looks like an advert from a magazine

Exercise 8

Ask students to work in small groups. Together, they should make one list of all the different types of social media platforms they use.

Then ask them to read the questions and deal with each media platform one by one.

EXTENSION Open up the discussion to the whole class, and encourage a representative from each group to summarize the key points.

PRE-WORK LEARNERS Students should be able to answer question 1 in connection with their place of study. For question 2, encourage students to share experiences of those companies which they have seen advertising on social media sites, and how they think the companies benefit.

Exercise 9

▶ 03 Students read questions 1-4 and then watch the third part of the interview.

After watching this part of the interview for the first time, draw students' attention to the *Glossary* of words and phrases. Don't check answers at this stage, as they will compare answers in **10**.

ALTERNATIVE With a weaker group, it might be useful to pause the video after each section.

Exercise 10

▶ 03 Students work in pairs to compare their answers to **9**. They then watch the video again and add to their notes.

Answers
1 Relatively, the ROI is better with social media.
2 With TV you have to pay for the reach, and the biggest TV audience on one day in the year is only equal to a social media audience every day.
3 Good social media advertising starts a conversation through interactivity and something thought-provoking. Now other forms of advertising try to start conversations in the same way or encourage interactivity.
4 A TV ad could be thought-provoking and so people talk about it on social media. Or a good billboard might get people to take photos and share them online.

Exercise 11

Students work in pairs and discuss the questions.

PRE-WORK LEARNERS Students could discuss how their college uses advertising and how the different forms – on- and offline – could work together synergistically. Alternatively, they could discuss their experiences of how one company uses, or could use, different forms of advertising synergistically.

EXTENSION Ask your students if, in their own non-work or non-study time, they are aware of post or re-post business adverts on social media, e.g. on Facebook, Twitter or Instagram, benefiting other companies.

Exercise 12

▶ 04 Students read the three points of consideration and then watch the final part of the interview to number the points in order.

Answers
1 b   2 c   3 a

Exercise 13

▶ 04 Students watch the video again and this time write down the questions to ask when planning each stage. Students can compare answers in pairs.

Answers
Content – what are you going to say?
Dissemination – how are you going to get that out there? Are you just going to sort of see it as advertising or are you going to try and get people to share it? How are you going to get it to spread?
Audience – who are you targeting? Are these existing customers? Are they potential customers? Are they both? What are their characteristics? Where do they live online? What do they do there?

Exercise 14

Ask students to work in groups. Together, they should choose an appropriate product or service to work on. They then discuss the three stages and consider the corresponding questions.

When they are ready, students present their new digital media strategy to the rest of the class. Encourage questions for clarification or more information.

ONE-TO-ONE Work together to decide which product or service to work on and help with brainstorming ideas. Then ask the student to present them.

Further ideas and video scripts

You can find a list of suggested ideas for how to use video in the class in the teacher resources in the *Online practice*. The video scripts are available to download from the Teaching resources on the Oxford Teachers' Club.
www.oup.com/elt/teacher/businessresult

Unit content

By the end of this unit, students will be able to
- talk about cultural differences
- describe past events and news
- describe the sequence of past events.

Context

In business, an awareness of the beliefs and values of cultures can be a crucial factor in the effectiveness of communication between two people from different countries. Even though two people may be speaking the same language, how that language (verbal and body) is used or interpreted can mean the difference between good or poor relationships.

The writer Geert Hofstede has researched and written about the behaviour of many cultures, and this unit includes a reading based on his work. Hofstede says that cultures have certain traits which, if we are aware of them, can help us to anticipate any possible difficulties. For example, someone from Malaysia will expect plenty of clear direction and control from management. However, someone from Denmark may expect much more freedom and involvement in the decision-making process. If two people from each of these cultures were expected to work together, there could be predictable consequences. For example, a Danish manager might choose to give an employee plenty of space for individual choice, but the Malaysian employee might interpret this to mean that the manager was not offering leadership or doing his or her job properly. For more on this topic, you or your students could search online for Hofstede's website, which includes a country-by-country analysis of culture.

In this unit, students discuss different cultural beliefs and values. They practise the language of narrating past events and review the relevant past tense grammar. In the *Talking point*, students look at how storytelling can be used effectively in business, and in talking about business.

Starting point

As you discuss these two questions, encourage students who regularly do business or work with people from different cultures to give real examples from their experience.

For question 2, if students have little experience of travelling, they can comment on how foreign visitors to their country behave.

In this lesson, it's important to note that discussion of culture and how other nationalities behave can be very sensitive. Inevitably, the topic lends itself to generalizations and one criticism of teaching 'cultural differences' is that we are prone to stereotyping the behaviour of different nationalities. Throughout this unit, steer conversations away from what might be interpreted as stereotyping or even prejudice.

Answers
1 The expression means that when you are in another country, you should behave like the people who live there. This might include eating the same food, wearing similar clothes and respecting local customs.
2 Answers will vary depending on the experience and attitude of your students.

Working with words

Exercise 1

Students could begin by brainstorming in small groups and then share their answers with the class. Write everyone's ideas on the board. Once you have listed the ideas on the board, students read the text and see if they are referred to (directly or indirectly).

Possible answers
how they greet people (shaking hands, bowing)
which gestures might be considered rude (showing the sole of your shoe in Arab countries)
some typical food dishes
their attitude to time (Do they like to be punctual or are they relaxed about time?)
whether small talk is important for relationship building (or if they like to get down to business quickly)
which topics you don't discuss (such as politics, sex, religion)
their view of work vs life (Is work more important than free time?)

Exercise 2

Students read again and identify the cultures.

Answers
1 collectivist (Korea, Colombia) and feminine (Sweden and Finland)
2 hierarchical (Malaysia, Indonesia) and cautious (Greece and Portugal)
3 risk-taking (Jamaica and Singapore)

Exercise 3

Students read the questions and discuss them as a class. They may need to read the text again to draw conclusions about their own culture. Open up the discussion to the class.

Exercise 4

Students work in pairs to match the adjectives and definitions.

Answers

1	formal	6	liberal
2	hierarchical	7	collectivist
3	egalitarian	8	strict
4	cautious	9	accepting
5	open	10	individualistic

PRONUNCIATION Read out the words in answers 1–10 and ask students to underline the stressed syllables (see Answers above).

Exercise 5

Note that the adjectives could be seen as positive or negative depending on your cultural viewpoint. For example, someone from the US may see traits such as *individualistic* as positive, whereas someone from Japan might take a more negative view. Typically, for a European student, you would expect that terms such as *open* and *liberal* would be positive.

Ask students to consider both views for each adjective.

For example, with *hierarchical*, the positive interpretation could be that a clear structure ensures that everyone knows where they stand and can aspire to climb the ladder; however, from a negative viewpoint, it could reinforce class differences and lead to low self-esteem in people at the bottom.

ALTERNATIVE Students first work alone to categorize the adjectives into *positive* or *negative*. Then they can compare their thoughts with a partner or in small groups. They should discuss the reasons for their difference in interpretation. For in-work students, ask them to comment on how they think their company culture would view the adjectives, e.g. does the company encourage individualism, collectivism or both?

Exercise 6

▶ **13.1** Students listen and answer the questions.

Answers

1 The first speaker stresses the importance of researching the local culture you're doing business with. The speaker's boss sold computers in the Middle East. He was familiar with the local culture and their way of doing business. He was competing against a US company with a better and cheaper product. However, the American representative did not do business in the way people were used to. So he lost the contract.
2 The second speaker is describing a course in understanding the culture of the place participants are going to work in. People learn about the political system, the social structure, basic cultural norms, taboo subjects, significant cultural differences between home and host country, and work culture.

ALTERNATIVE ▶ **13.1** To help weaker students, you could give them a more focused listening task. Write these questions on the board (answers are shown in brackets):

Speaker 1

1 *According to the speaker, what is essential for business success?* (To be informed about the culture and be tolerant.)
2 *What main advantage did his boss have over the competitor?* (He had been there for a few years and was familiar with the country.)
3 *In what way was the American both good and bad at his job?* (He had a better product at a better price and could give presentations, but he didn't understand the need for long relationship building in the Middle East.)

Speaker 2

4 *What kind of companies and industries do participants come from?* (telecoms, engineering, computers, banking)
5 *What does the company hope is the outcome of their courses?* (Participants will be more sensitive and their colleagues from other cultures will have more respect for them).

Exercise 7

Students complete the sentences and can compare answers in pairs.

Answers

1	sensitive	5	respectful
2	adjust	6	informed
3	familiar	7	used
4	aware	8	tolerant

DICTIONARY SKILLS
To complete **7**, it would be helpful for students to realize that all eight words are typically followed by a particular preposition, e.g. *sensitive to*, *familiar with*. A good dictionary contains this information. Show this to students and let them check their answers in **7** using a dictionary.

Exercise 8

Students make five questions about cross-cultural understanding. You could help with the following examples:
Are you aware of different ways in which cultures can greet each other?
Do you think it's important to be sensitive to foreign visitors' eating requirements?
Are you very familiar with one particular culture?
Is it important to be especially respectful of older people in your culture?
Would you describe your country as tolerant of different cultures?
Are people in your country informed or trained about other cultures they deal with?
Do you find it easy to adjust to a new country?
Are you used to dealing with people from other countries?

In pairs, students ask and answer their questions. Alternatively, students can work in pairs to prepare their questions and then ask and answer with another pair.

Further practice

If students need more practice, go to *Practice file 13* on page 130 of the *Student's Book*.

Exercise 9

Students will need 10–15 minutes to prepare their list of ideas for each item. Encourage them to mention the key cultural factors in the article and explain how they might affect behaviour. Afterwards, they can either present their ideas to the whole class or to another pair.

Give positive feedback on vocabulary used from this section.

PRE-WORK LEARNERS Ask students to imagine an overseas student coming to their college or joining their course. They could consider the following issues: relationships between students and staff; policies on attendance, assignments and deadlines; social events; etc.

> **EXTRA ACTIVITY**
> As a follow-up, which can be done in class or for homework, students write a short leaflet for colleagues who come on six-month secondments from overseas to work in their company. It should cover similar information to that in **9**.

Photocopiable worksheet

Download and photocopy *Unit 13 Working with words* worksheet from the teacher resources in the *Online practice*.

Business communication

Exercise 1

Before you start, ask students to read the *Context* to find out what 'critical incidents' are. Also mention that critical incidents are often used on training courses in intercultural awareness; course participants discuss these in groups.

You might be interested to read *Intercultural Business Communication* by Robert Gibson (2002, Oxford University Press). It contains a number of these critical incidents for intercultural training purposes.

▶ **13.2** Before you play the listening, check understanding of the term *loss of face* in situation 5 (= being less respected or looking stupid because of something you have done).

> **Answers**
> Conversation 1: 3, 5
> Conversation 2: 2, 3

> **EXTRA ACTIVITY**
> Ask students if they have come across similar incidents where issues of seniority, asking questions or loss of face have been critical factors.

Exercise 2

▶ **13.2** Students listen again and complete the sentences.

> **Answers**
>
> | | |
> |---|---|
> | 1 As time went by | 6 but then |
> | 2 That was when | 7 So that was |
> | 3 that's | 8 So what |
> | 4 it wasn't until | 9 in the end |
> | 5 due to | 10 It came about because of |

Exercise 3

Students categorize sentences 1–10 in **2**.

> **Answers**
> a 1, 2, 4, 6, 7, 9
> b 5, 10
> c 3, 8

Refer students to the *Tip* when you are checking answers for category b.

> **EXTRA ACTIVITY**
> In category c, there are two examples of how a listener can encourage the speaker. Showing you are listening like this is an important communication skill. Ask students to find more examples of these kinds of phrases in audio script 13.2 on page 152 of the *Student's Book*, e.g. *Yeah … / Oh? / Go on … / What had you done? / I see. / So you mean …? / What happened? / And …?* Note that students focused on this feature in **5** in *Unit 2*, on page 15 of the *Student's Book*.

Further practice

If students need more practice, go to *Practice file 13* on page 130 of the *Student's Book*.

Exercise 4

Students need to read the text about Indonesia first to help them understand the cultural error in the pictures. Then students study the pictures and prepare a narrative of the critical incident. They need to combine phrases from the *Key expressions* and the prompts below each picture.

EXTENSION Students change partners and take turns telling the story to each other. The listening student must use phrases to show they are listening (see previous *Extra activity*).

Exercise 5

After both students have discussed a situation, ask for a volunteer to tell their story to the rest of the class. Comment on use of phrases and how students structured their stories.

Photocopiable worksheet

Download and photocopy *Unit 13 Business communication* worksheet from the teacher resources in the *Online practice*.

Practically speaking

Exercise 1

Students read the questions and share their ideas with a partner or in a small group. Elicit one or two ideas.

Exercise 2

▶ **13.3** Students listen and identify the topic of each conversation.

> **Answers**
> a conversation 3
> b conversation 2
> c conversation 1

Exercise 3

▶ **13.3** Before you start, check *rumour* – a piece of news passed from person to person, that may or may not be true.

Answers
a 4, 8, 10
b 1, 3, 5, 7, 9
c 2, 6

Exercise 4

If students have problems thinking of news items, write the following on the board for ideas to use with the phrases:

- *job losses at your foreign subsidiary*
- *colleague crashed the company car*
- *colleague forgot his/her passport when going on an important business trip*
- *two colleagues are getting married – no one knew they were a couple*
- *project manager in trouble – miscalculated costs and is already in the red*
- *company is relocating to new, state-of-the-art office building*

PRE-WORK LEARNERS Students can think of news where they study. Students could also make up one of the pieces of news. The other student has to guess which piece of news is true and which is made up.

Language at work

Exercise 1

As a lead-in, ask students to close their books and write the following words randomly around the board.

American billionaire   Christmas   flat tyre   flowers   wife   mortgage

Tell students that these words come from a real story. They work in pairs to predict what happens in the story using the words. After a few minutes, ask for suggestions. Students finally read the story on page 90 of the *Student's Book*.

Afterwards, ask students if they think the story is true, and to discuss their ideas and reasons with a partner.

Exercise 2

Students read the sentences and then number the events in the order in which they happened.

Note that in this activity, students may be tempted to simply order the events in the order they appear in the story itself. However, the idea is that the events are numbered as they really happened so, for example, sentence e *The chauffeur didn't put the tool kit in the boot*, is listed later in the article but in reality was the first event because of the use of the past perfect in the text.

Answers
a 6 **b** 3 **c** 2 **d** 4 **e** 1 **f** 8 **g** 5 **h** 9 **i** 7

Exercise 3

Refer students to the *Language point*. Students begin by underlining the verbs. They then complete the explanations with the correct narrative tense.

Answers
1 Past continuous: was being driven, was raining, were leaving, was standing, was leaving
Past simple: was, got, pulled over, opened, realized, saw, stopped, changed, wound down, asked, could, said, arrived
Past perfect: had left, had been paid off
2 Use the Past continuous to describe the background information at the beginning of the story.
Use the Past simple to describe the main actions and events in the story.
Use the Past continuous to talk about an action in progress, interrupted by another action.
Use the Past perfect to talk about an action that happened before another past action.

Grammar reference

If students need more information, go to *Grammar reference* on page 131 of the *Student's Book*.

Exercise 4

Students complete the sentences with the correct form of the verbs.

Answers
1 was snowing, slept
2 was talking, sent
3 had forgotten, apologized
4 was staying, decided
5 was leaving, gave
6 had lost, wore

Further practice

If students need more practice, go to *Practice file 13* on page 131 of the *Student's Book*.

Exercise 5

Allow students a few minutes to prepare their stories or an idea of their own. They might find it helpful to list the events and then think about how they could give background information with the past continuous, or how they could show one event happening before another with the past perfect. Comment on the content of the story, then for language feedback, focus on use of these past tenses.

EXTRA ACTIVITY
Your students might find it useful to write down their stories; this will also allow you to assess their ability to produce narrative tenses correctly.

You could suggest they write a first draft of their story, then show it to a partner (swap stories). They should give each other feedback on the story itself and, if appropriate with your students, make comments on use of narrative tenses. They then swap back and revise their texts.

If students can do this writing on a laptop or tablet, revising and writing a second draft will be very quick and easy.

Photocopiable worksheet

Download and photocopy *Unit 13 Language at work* worksheet from the teacher resources in the *Online practice*.

Talking point

Discussion

Exercise 1

Students read the question and discuss it with a partner. Encourage them to think of specific examples and share their ideas with the class.

Then ask students to read the text.

Exercise 2

▶ 13.4 Students read the questions and then listen to someone talking about the history of a company in two different ways. They can share their opinions with a partner.

EXTENSION Ask students to discuss in pairs what made the two stories different. Elicit some of their ideas.

Exercise 3

You could ask students to work in different pairs for this.

If it helps, ask students to write down key words from the first story. They then work with a partner to retell it.

▶ 13.4 Students listen to the first version of the story again and compare it to their own. Was there anything they forgot?

EXTRA ACTIVITY

Ask students to read the audio script on page 152 of the *Student's Book*, and find any phrases which they think contribute to the success of the first version of the story, e.g.:

Everything they knew …

News of … spread and …

up and down the state …

In the end, …

the whole of the USA …

… still continue to this day

Suggest they think of other similar phrases and try to include some of these into their own stories in the *Task* to make their stories easier to follow, and more interesting to listen to.

Task

Exercise 1

Students work alone to plan a story about their own company, or a company they know well. Remind them to include all the information and to focus less on facts and figures, and more on the human side of the company and its culture. Give them about ten minutes. They should make notes only, not write down full sentences.

PRE-WORK LEARNERS Students could choose a company they know something about, and do some mini-research online. They could bring the information to the next class in preparation for telling their stories.

Exercise 2

Students work in groups. They will be retelling each other's stories and, at the end, they will compare the original with the final version. The 'owner' of each story will be particularly interested to see if and how it changes.

ONE-TO-ONE An alternative way to organize this would be to each make clear notes of the story of the company on paper. You then tell each other's stories, using the information, but trying to convey the key information and company culture in an interesting way. As you each listen to the information about your company, make a note in your mind of anything that is narrated differently. It will be interesting to discuss these aspects afterwards.

Exercise 3

Ask students to work with a partner. They should think about which parts of the stories they found most interesting, and why. Elicit some of their ideas.

EXTENSION Ask your students to think about when they can use such mini-stories in their work or studies, e.g. in a presentation, in a blog post, when meeting new people (open days, trade fairs, conferences), etc.

Progress test

Download and photocopy *Unit 13 Progress test* and *Speaking test* from the teacher resources in the *Online practice*.

14 Performance

Unit content

By the end of this unit, students will be able to
- talk about appraisals
- evaluate performance and raise issues
- talk about imagined past actions and results.

Context

There are a number of steps a company must take to understand if it is performing well. Firstly, it has to create standards by which performance is measured. Then it must measure performance using the criteria in order to analyse or evaluate the results. Either the standards are met or they are not and action may be required.

For many companies, the criteria for assessing performance will be based on financial information. Typically, the amount of profit made in a year is indicative of whether a company is performing well. However, financial results do not tell the whole story and could be misleading. We can also measure performance in other areas such as the performance of staff. This kind of information can be crucial to long-term success, though it may be somewhat harder to evaluate objectively or meaningfully.

Such is the importance of performance in modern business thinking that it has given rise to its own concept. 'Performance management' is about managing staff so that they know what is expected of them. Staff are trained in the skills that will help them to deliver, and the company must create a culture of openness where staff feel free to discuss and contribute to individual and team aims and objectives.

In this unit, students begin by considering performance in terms of staff and the process of staff appraisals. They practise the language for discussing and evaluating performance supported by a language section on third/mixed conditionals and past modals. In the *Talking point*, they read about competition in the workplace: how it can be both advantageous and cause problems. They then consider how to involve healthy competition in a workplace situation.

Starting point

Discuss the first question as a class. Alternatively, divide the class into three groups and assign an area to each group. Each group brainstorms a list of criteria and then reports back. Write any ideas on the board.

For questions 2 and 3, it will be helpful for students to refer back to the ideas on the board from question 1.

Possible answers

1   Company: This is usually based on financial information such as turnover, and profit and loss. It could also consider figures relating to productivity or speed at which raw materials are turned into the finished product.
Project: This is often assessed on budget (over or under), effective use of resources and if it is completed on time.
Employee: Employees are measured by criteria which are often subjective, such as how well the employee works with other members of a team. However, in some jobs such as sales which are results driven, it is easier to assess performance by the number of units sold. Similarly, staff can also be measured in terms of timekeeping and attendance.
2   Students' own answers
3   Any criteria which involve figures or analysis of financial results will be easier to measure.

PRE-WORK LEARNERS Students can talk about how their performance is measured or assessed at their place of study.

Working with words

Exercise 1

Check that students understand the concept of *staff appraisal*. If any of them have experience of appraisals, either leading or taking one, ask for a brief description of what happens.

Ask them to read the questions and share their experiences in pairs. Elicit some ideas to share with the group.

PRE-WORK LEARNERS If not already discussed, students can talk about how their performance is measured or assessed at their place of study. What different methods are used?

Exercise 2

Students read the questions and then read the text to find the answers.

Answers

2   In one survey of 2,900 workers, 29% thought annual appraisals were a waste of time. 21% even described them as 'unfair'. Many more were positive about the experience but felt that receiving constructive feedback on a more regular basis would be more beneficial.
3   General Electric uses an app to get regularly updated feedback. Adobe uses frequent face-to-face check-ins.

Exercise 3

Students read the questions and share any ideas they have about the approaches to appraisals with a partner. Then open up the discussion to the class.

PRE-WORK LEARNERS Ask students to consider how they would feel about the General Electric and/or Adobe approaches to feedback and assessment at their school or college. Would they consider giving or receiving feedback via an app to or from their tutor? What sorts of issues might be appropriate or inappropriate to 'discuss' in this way? How would students feel about regular face-to-face check-ins with their tutors or supervisors?

Exercise 4

Students match a verb from A to a noun (phrase) in B, and refer to the text to check their answers. The answers for this exercise are included after **5**.

Exercise 5

Students use the phrases they made in **4** to match to the definitions.

Answers
1 conduct annual appraisals
2 express views
3 address concerns
4 receive constructive feedback
5 rate objectives on a scale
6 monitor performance
7 agree objectives
8 respond to criticism
9 raise issues

PRONUNCIATION Ask students to pick out any words with three or four syllables and underline the stressed syllable.

Answers
appra<u>i</u>sal, con<u>struc</u>tive, ob<u>jec</u>tives, <u>mon</u>itor, per<u>for</u>mance, <u>cri</u>ticism

Exercise 6

Students make questions with phrases from **5**. To help students with this task, write an example question on the board, e.g. *How do you agree performance objectives with your manager?*

Students write the questions on their own and then pair up to ask each other. They could then report back on their findings to another pair or to the whole class.

PRE-WORK LEARNERS Ask students to think about how an ideal appraisal system might work at a company, and to write questions, using the phrases in **5**, to ask and answer about this, e.g.:
Do you use any online means of receiving constructive feedback?
How are employees encouraged to respond to criticism?
What means are there for employees to raise issues?

Exercise 7

▶ 14.1 It may be helpful to clarify the meaning of *top-down appraisal* before focusing on *360-degree feedback*. The appraisal described in the reading is *top-down* and basically means that a manager talks to the employee about how he or she is doing. Following this, before listening, ask students if they have heard of or can guess what *360-degree feedback* refers to.

You may need to clarify *suitable counselling*: giving feedback and advice sensitively and constructively.

Answers
1 360-degree feedback is a development tool. Employees assess themselves using a form and several other people – manager, colleagues, anyone they work closely with – also give feedback using the same form. This gives a more complete picture of how someone is doing.
2 job skills, abilities, attitudes and behaviour
3 It has to be completely confidential and suitable counselling should be available when you go through the feedback results.

Exercise 8

Draw students' attention to the fact that they are making noun + noun phrases with these words.

Answers
1 appraisal   4 rating
2 tool   5 judgement
3 criteria   6 management

Exercise 9

Students ask and answer the questions in **8**. They may need to refer back to the information in audio script 14.1 on page 153 of the *Student's Book* to answer some of these questions. They will need to summarize key points in some of their answers.

PRE-WORK LEARNERS Use the following alternative questions:

4 What opportunities are there for peer rating in your school or college? Would this be appropriate when working on assignments? Who would do this in your context?
5 If you were rating a peer's assignment, how honest would you be in your value judgement of your peers?
6 Do you, or any of your peers, have a role in supporting other peers, perhaps students from abroad, or those who are newer to their courses?

Exercise 10

Students can do this in pairs. When they make sentences with the phrasal verbs, it might be helpful for them to think of an appraisal process where they work. For example: *You end up with a clear idea of your targets.*

Answers
1 end up with   4 hand out
2 come over   5 go through
3 move on   6 carry on

PRE-WORK LEARNERS Students could use the phrasal verbs in the context of receiving exam results, an end-of-term report or feedback from their teacher. For example: *The teacher hands out the exam paper. Afterwards, we go through the answers together.*

Further practice

If students need more practice, go to *Practice file 14* on page 132 of the *Student's Book*.

Exercise 11

Students can work in pairs. It might be useful to work through an example with the class first. For example:

Doctor

Job skills: knowledge of science/medicine and how the body works, diagnostic and surgery skills; ability to respond to patients' questions, put them at ease and discuss their concerns.

People involved would include: colleagues, administrative staff, senior and junior doctors; nurses; lab staff; patients; patients' relatives, etc.

During the discussion, prompt students with vocabulary from the section. Students could make a list and tick a word/phrase every time they manage to use it.

PRE-WORK LEARNERS Students could choose one of the following jobs, or a different job they know something about, e.g. teacher, salesperson, accountant.

Photocopiable worksheet

Download and photocopy *Unit 14 Working with words* worksheet from the teacher resources in the *Online practice*.

Business communication

Exercise 1

Students read the *Context* and discuss the question with a partner. Elicit one or two ideas to share with the class.

Exercise 2

▶ 14.2 Ask students to look at the headings and information required in the table. Students listen to complete the table.

Answers

	Appraisee feedback	Appraiser comments	Action to be taken
Positive achievements	1 helping to produce the in-house magazine	1 demonstrated great prioritizing skills, even with tight deadlines 2 move to new office went very smoothly	
Areas for improvement / development	1 to improve chances of working with international colleagues 2 no other areas need improving on	1 sign up for a language course 2 need to focus on gaining more qualifications	1/2 language course and management course to be put on lists of goals for coming year

Areas of concern	1 too much work with magazine project 2 found it difficult to delegate 3 would have been better to take the old rota to the new location	1 shouldn't have been expected to take on so much 2 – 3 the call centre rota – there has been negative feedback	1 let them know if it happens again 2 – 3 arrange a meeting to discuss it next week
Resources required	1 training on the new program 2 some new software	1 A to check the budget 2 T to put request in email	

Exercise 3

Students work in pairs to decide who said the phrases.

Exercise 4

▶ 14.2 Students listen again to check their answers to **3**.

Answers
1 A 2 T 3 A 4 A 5 T 6 A 7 A 8 T 9 T 10 T

With sentence 6 in **3**, refer students to the *Tip*. Note that it isn't enough to add emphasis by simply including the word in a sentence. It also has to be stressed. It may be helpful to drill students with the three sentences given in the *Tip* and make sure they stress the words in bold (*really*, *certainly*, *I must say*).

Exercise 5

Students put the phrases from **3** into the six categories.

Answers
a 4, 7   b 1, 3   c 2   d 6, 8   e 5   f 9, 10

Refer students to the *Key expressions*. They could compare their answers to **5** here. You could ask them to choose one or two expressions from each category that they think would be useful for them to use.

Further practice

If students need more practice, go to *Practice file 14* on page 132 of the *Student's Book*.

Exercise 6

Students read the five points and think of one, two or three examples for each one. Remind them that they can invent information if they prefer.

You could elicit or give an example first, e.g.:

Something you've enjoyed, or that worked well, e.g. *working with my new colleague Alex: we've both learnt a lot from each other*.

Something you are concerned about, e.g. *I've got a lot of work trips coming up over the next few months, and I don't know how I'm going to be able to do all my regular work as well*.

PRE-WORK LEARNERS Students should still be able to do this task, in relation to their studies, or any part-time employment they have had.

Exercise 7

Students work in pairs. They'll be using phrases from the *Key expressions* to find out more information about their partner's points in **6**. Students tell each other the key information they noted down for each point in **6**: their partner notes down the information in the table in the first column, and uses phrases and questions to comment on these (second column). Finally, students agree on the action to be taken (third column).

ALTERNATIVE If you have a weaker group, ask students first to note down each other's comments in **6** in the first column. They then work alone to decide which phrases would be most appropriate to respond to those, and write them down in the second column. They could then discuss this.

Monitor for correct use of phrases in the *Key expressions*. You could then lead a discussion about what makes a good appraisal. Ask them to comment on their partner's performance as the appraiser, as it's a particularly difficult task, e.g. *Was their partner tactful? Did they make them feel motivated?*

Photocopiable worksheet
Download and photocopy *Unit 14 Business communication* worksheet from the teacher resources in the *Online practice*.

Practically speaking

Exercise 1

Students work in pairs and read the questions and the three situations. Give them four or five minutes to discuss what they have done, or would do. You could elicit a few ideas and compare them with the whole class.

Exercise 2

▶ 14.3 Students listen to the conversation, match them to one of the situations in **1**, and say how each employee reacts. Students can compare their answers with a partner.

Answers
Conversation 1: There has been a complaint about an employee from a colleague in the same office – the employee reacts angrily.
Conversation 2: An employee is going to be made redundant because of restructuring – the employee had expected it and seems resigned to the news.

Exercise 3

▶ 14.3 Students read the phrases and then listen again to order them.

Answers
1 I'm going to get straight to the point.
2 I've received a complaint about you.
3 Before we go any further …
4 I'd like to hear your side of the story.
5 There's something we need to discuss.
6 This is rather delicate, but …
7 I realize it isn't easy for you to hear this …
8 It wasn't an easy decision to make.
9 We don't have much choice.

EXTENSION Ask students if they can think of any other phrases they could use in these situations, e.g. *I'm afraid …; I'd like to talk to you about something; There's an awkward issue we need to discuss.*

EXTRA ACTIVITY
For situations where a feedback or review meeting hasn't been specifically arranged, ask students to think of the other matters to bear in mind when raising difficult issues with a colleague, employee or peer, e.g. where the conversation takes place, at what time of day, etc. This should help ensure that the 'receiver' is in the best position to be told the information, and to think about how to respond. For example, a 'chance' meeting just before lunch in the corridor might be very unsuitable. However, an email or short message to set up a meeting could be appropriate. Ask students what times and places would or wouldn't be appropriate in their culture.

Exercise 4

Students role-play each of the situations in **1**, using the phrases from **3**. You could ask them to work with a new partner for each situation.

Language at work

Exercise 1

Students read the sentences and decide what has or hasn't happened in each one.

Answers
1 Katy has left. The speaker didn't do the course.
2 The other person didn't think enough about the rota.
3 The person didn't start the language course and isn't proficient.
4 The other person didn't do the course.

Exercise 2

Ask students to read the *Language point* and the information, and to choose a sentence from **1** to complete the explanations.

Answers
a 1   b 3   c 2   d 4

Grammar reference
If students need more information, go to *Grammar reference* on page 133 of the *Student's Book*.

Exercise 3

Students read and discuss the questions, and find the answers in the sentences in **1**.

Answers
Sentence 1: (third conditional): past perfect / *would have* + past participle
Sentence 3: (mixed conditional): past perfect / *would* + *be*
Sentence 2: *might have* could replace *could have*
Sentence 4: *ought to have* could replace *should have*

Further practice

If students need more practice, go to *Practice file 14* on page 133 of the *Student's Book*.

Exercise 4

Students work with a partner and read the two situations. They should discuss what they could say in each one. Check their use of the conditionals. You could recap on these, for each half of the sentence, with the following questions: *Is the situation real or imaginary? Is it now or in the past? Can you change what happened? Can you change the situation now?*

Possible answers

1 If I had waited to get authorization for the car, I would have been late for the meeting. If I'd been late for the meeting, we might have lost the contract. If we had lost the contract, the company wouldn't be expanding now.
2 If we hadn't used our regular supplier, we would have got a discount. But if we had used the new supplier, they might not have delivered on time. And if they hadn't delivered on time, we wouldn't have enough paper for the current mailshot.

EXTRA ACTIVITY

If you feel students need more practice with the target structures in **2**, write this scenario on the board for them to discuss in a similar way.

Your company invested heavily in a small company in South America. The South American company went bankrupt. Your company lost a substantial amount of money. Present result: your company is scaling back and making people redundant.

Exercise 5

Students read the situations and then decide how they could respond. There are various ways, so encourage students to suggest more than one way.

Possible answers

1 You should have been more polite in the letter.
2 You could have let me know!
3 You should have checked with the manager.
4 You should have told me about the change.
5 You could have lost your job over that.

Exercise 6

Allow students a few minutes to read the four topics, and to think about what they could say in each one.

This is the first opportunity for students to use third and mixed conditionals more freely, so expect to correct verb forms used by students during the conversations.

PRE-WORK LEARNERS Instead of the first bullet point, you could ask students to think about why they chose their particular subject or course.

Photocopiable worksheet

Download and photocopy *Unit 14 Language at work* worksheet from the teacher resources in the *Online practice*.

Talking point

Discussion

Exercise 1

Before asking students to read the text, you could ask them to look at the headline and share any thoughts they have from their own experience, or from stories they have heard.

Students read the questions and then the text to find the answers.

Answers

Initially, staff were motivated to be better than those in other teams; it was probably fun at first, and participants were perhaps more interested in the competition element than in the improvements at work.

Exercise 2

Students read the first part of the question about negative consequences, and find the answer in the text. They then read the second question and think of other disadvantages, e.g. some teams might be stronger than others, so always win; this will be demotivating for other groups who consider it unlikely they can beat them; employees focus more on the competition and lose sight of important aspects of the work itself. This could lead to shortcuts and a lower quality of goods or services.

Answers

The leader of the successful team resigned and took most of his team members with him to start a rival company.

Exercise 3

Students share their experiences about competition in the workplace, and how it could be effective in their company.

PRE-WORK LEARNERS Students can consider competition at school/college.

Task

Exercise 1

Ask students to work in small groups. Ask them to read the situation and the questions. You could ask them first to work in groups and brainstorm different ways of improving staff performance. When they have three or more, ask them to think about the issues in the questions in relation to each idea.

Exercise 2

If you have a small class, groups can present to the whole class. Otherwise, put groups together to compare their ideas.

Encourage students listening to ask questions for clarification. You could have a class vote on the best and fairest way to introduce competition in this situation.

Progress test

Download and photocopy *Unit 14 Progress test* and *Speaking test* from the teacher resources in the *Online practice*.

Unit content

By the end of this unit, students will be able to

- talk about career breaks
- present a case
- talk about time off
- discuss interview questions.

Context

The 'career break' is a relatively modern concept and not necessarily one that will be familiar to students from all parts of the world. There are also different levels of career break. For example, someone might take a break for personal or family reasons, such as to have children, before returning to the same (or a similar) job some months or years later. However, the notion of 'gap years' for professional people has also become acceptable in some businesses. After working for a number of years, a person can request extended time off or a 'sabbatical'. This could be to travel round parts of the world or to take an extended holiday. In fact, some research now suggests that companies offering career breaks are able to recruit and keep good staff. It is estimated that one in five UK companies have career break policies. This trend has been aided by the increase in companies which specialize in arranging gap years.

Many professionals also make use of their skills during a career break and do voluntary work for an organization such as an NGO (non-governmental organization) in the developing world. The advantage of this is that they are actively enhancing their CV and future employers are more likely to look favourably on this kind of career break experience.

This unit begins by looking at examples of career breaks where people travelled or were involved in overseas projects. Students consider the pros and cons of taking such a break before presenting their own idea for a personal break. In *Business communication*, they practise the language for presenting a case in the context of convincing others about a break from work. In the *Talking point*, students look at a programme which organizes a one-year break where participants continue working for their company. They then set up role-play situations to interview potential candidates.

Starting point

Ask students what they think a career break is. Then, if needed, provide a definition: *career break* – a period of time when you do not do your usual job, either with or without the support of your employer, for example, because you have children to care for or want to study.

Students could discuss question 1 with a partner and then you could open up the discussion to the whole class.

For question 2, you could brainstorm ideas as a class. You could put these on the board as they may be useful to refer to later.

Possible answer

2 For the employee, the career break will be expensive and the person will need to anticipate reduced (or no) earnings and therefore a change in their spending. They may also find that they miss the routine more than they expected. Ideally, the employee will take the break and return to the same employer. However, this means the employer needs someone to temporarily replace the person and possibly to pay for retraining.

PRE-WORK LEARNERS If you are teaching students in a college or university, it is possible that some of them will have taken a gap year after school. Ask them to tell the class briefly the kind of gap year it was and what they think the benefits were.

Working with words

Exercise 1

As a fun lead-in, offering further speaking practice, put students into groups of three. Each student in the group chooses to be one of the three people on page 98 of the *Student's Book* (Freya, Roberto or Jenny). Students have two minutes to read and memorize the information about their character. Then they close their books. Each student briefly summarizes who they are and what they have done. The two listening students make notes about this person. When everyone has spoken, students read all three profiles on page 98 and check how comprehensive and correct their notes were.

Set a time limit of about three minutes for students to read the texts and answer 1–5. Avoid dealing with too much unknown vocabulary at this stage. Tell students to underline the parts of the text which helped them answer, and ask them to say what these were when you check answers.

Answers

1 Roberto and Jenny (South-east Asia and Bangladesh), Roberto and Freya (Australia)
2 Roberto and Jenny (both employers 'kept the job open')
3 Freya and Roberto (make sure you've got good career experience before you leave / take it after you've worked for five years)
4 Freya and Jenny (voluntary work in Australia / worked with local communities to improve education and healthcare)
5 Freya and Jenny (it has given me a new perspective / it broadened my outlook)

Exercise 2

Students discuss the question in pairs and then report back to the rest of the class.

Exercise 3

Students find the pairs of words with similar meanings.

> **Answers**
> perspective / outlook
> hesitating / feeling uncertain
> piece of advice / tip
> put off / postponed
> appreciate / feel grateful for
> voluntary organization / charity

PRONUNCIATION Ask students to identify words in **3** with:

- three syllables (*perspective*, *voluntary*, *charity*)
- four syllables (*hesitating*, *appreciate*)
- five syllables (*organization*).

They should also mark the word stress. Note that students might query the pronunciation of *voluntary* /ˈvɒləntri/ on the final syllable. It looks like it should be two syllables, not one.

Exercise 4

Note that in some cases, both synonyms can be used. However, in sentence 2, *recharged* would sound slightly odd as we tend to use it as a metaphor with the word *batteries*.

> **Answers**
> 1 voluntary organization / charity
> 2 revitalized / recharged
> 3 put off / postpone
> 4 perspective / outlook
> 5 appreciate / feel grateful for
> 6 piece of advice / tip

Exercise 5

Students ask each other the questions in **4**. At the end, ask each pair to report back on their answers to two of the questions.

Exercise 6

▶ **15.1** Before listening, ask students to read the questions and to suggest what they think the term *flexiwork* might refer to. (*Flexiwork* means the practice of being able to work when you want to, e.g. working intensively for three months and then taking a break for three months. It isn't the same as being freelance because you keep a contract with the company.)

> **Answers**
> 1 because the industry was having a bit of a downturn
> 2 because a lot of their work is project-based and consultants work for different lengths of time on projects
> 3 cost savings, improves staff retention rate, a chance for staff to broaden horizons, a way to attract new staff
> 4 The employee learns new skills which the company also benefits from. He or she also has renewed motivation.

Exercise 7

Students can underline the correct words in the questionnaire.

> **Answers**
> 1 off
> 2 soft
> 3 renewed
> 4 broaden
> 5 development
> 6 policy
> 7 retention

Exercise 8

Students respond to the questionnaire in **7** in relation to their working situation.

PRE-WORK LEARNERS Students answer questions 1–4 only, as these will apply to most people.

Further practice

If students need more practice, go to *Practice file 15* on page 134 of the *Student's Book*.

Exercise 9

Students can do this alone or in pairs. The presentations can be given in small groups or to the whole class. It's probably useful to set a time limit of two minutes. Explain that they only have this amount of time to convince the other people listening. When everyone has given a presentation, the class could vote on which was the most convincing.

Give extra positive feedback to any student who managed to use lots of the vocabulary from this section.

PRE-WORK LEARNERS As a variation to **9**, tell students that they plan to take a gap year when they finish their current studies. They need to convince their parents and they will also need to borrow some money from them. Students prepare their ideas, remembering they will need to talk about the benefits and financial arrangements. Finally, students can give their presentations to the class. Or you could set up a role-play situation where one student plays the part of the parent, who must be convinced by the other student.

Photocopiable worksheet

Download and photocopy *Unit 15 Working with words* worksheet from the teacher resources in the *Online practice*.

Business communication

Exercise 1

As a lead-in, ask students to suggest situations in which they might need to present a personal case: for example, at a job interview; when they have been criticized for something (by a customer); to suggest a new innovation or idea.

▶ **15.2** Students need to study the *Context*, which is a profile of Lena, and the notes giving possible reasons for a career break. Before they listen, discuss which of the reasons listed are likely to convince an employer. For example, *I'm feeling burnt-out!* might be true but may not be so convincing. When checking answers, note that Lena does mention advertising opportunities but these relate to her company sponsoring her exhibition afterwards, not her trip.

> **Answers**
> I've been a loyal employee.
> I'll feel more settled and focused after the trip.
> I'll gain experience I can bring to the company.
> It's a lifelong ambition of mine.

Exercise 2

▶ **15.2** Students listen again and number the phrases in the order in which they hear them.

> **Answers**
> **a** 3 **b** 7 **c** 8 **d** 1 **e** 2 **f** 6 **g** 9 **h** 4 **i** 5

With sentence i, refer students to the *Tip* about *valuable* and *invaluable*.

Exercise 3

Students match the underlined words in sentences 1–9 to phrases a–i in **2** with the same meaning.

> **Answers**
> **2** e **3** a **4** h **5** i **6** f **7** b **8** c **9** g

Refer students to the *Key expressions*. Ask them to find one from each pair of sentences in their answers to **3**, and find the category it belongs to.

> **Further practice**
> If students need more practice, go to *Practice file 15* on page 134 of the *Student's Book*.

Exercise 4

Students work in pairs and follow the instructions given. As they prepare their arguments, monitor each pair and check they have followed the structure for presenting their case. Also remind them to make use of the phrases from the *Key expressions* at each stage. Note that this is meant as controlled practice, and students talk through their case and arguments with another pair – they don't have to actually present the case. However, you could ask them to go on and role-play the situation instead of doing the freer practice in **5** and **6**.

Ask students to say which students' arguments were particularly convincing, and why. What strategies did they use? Comment and give feedback on each pair's use of phrases.

Exercise 5

This offers freer practice with the language in this section. Students work on their own and choose one of the ideas or an idea of their own. They then prepare their case. Remind them to refer back to the stages in **4**, i.e. to plan what they are going to say, anticipate what objectives there may be and think about appropriate phrases to use. Allow students enough time to prepare their case before they present to a partner.

PRE-WORK LEARNERS Students could choose one of the following ideas: implement a new system for evaluating students (e.g. not just based on exams, but from assessing coursework, too); introduce a new method of receiving feedback (e.g. from peers as well as tutors; or online, to make revisions or second drafts easier to work on); add in field-work or trips to the course to see how their studies will be useful in real life.

Exercise 6

Students work in pairs to present their case. Their partner plays the role of their boss.

If you feel that after the first situation, students still need more practice with the language, then ask them to choose another situation and repeat the task. They could do this with a different partner.

> **Photocopiable worksheet**
> Download and photocopy *Unit 15 Business communication* worksheet from the teacher resources in the *Online practice*.

Practically speaking

Exercise 1

As a lead-in, ask each student to say what they did last weekend and write activities on the board. Find out if this is typical of how they spend their time off from work. This will help set the scene for the section and the activity in **3**.

▶ **15.3** Students listen and identify what each speaker did during their time off.

> **Answers**
> **1** did DIY
> **2** hiked in the Swiss Alps
> **3** visited partner's family

DIY means 'Do-It-Yourself' and refers to decorating and carrying out improvements to your house. The DIY business in places such as the UK has grown hugely in recent decades. However, it is not a typical free-time activity in all countries, so may need to be explained.

Exercise 2

▶ **15.3** Students read the questions and phrases, and then listen again to match the questions and phrases a–i to the conversations in **1**.

> **Answers**
> 1 c, e, f
> 2 a, d, i
> 3 b, g, h

You may need to clarify the following in conversation 1:

to take (a day) off = to have a free day from work

to get up to = to be busy with something

ALTERNATIVE Ask students to read the questions and phrases and try to match them to the conversations before listening again. They then listen to check.

Exercise 3

It will help if students stand up for this activity so they can easily move from one person to the next. Students can refer back to the ideas for free time on the board (see lead-in idea in **1**) if they want to invent information.

When they have finished, you could ask students to report back on any especially interesting ways they have, or have heard about, for spending time off (real or invented).

ONE-TO-ONE Give your student time to think about or invent examples. You could simply have a conversation about these, along with your own examples, or for the second and third conversations, one of you could take on a different role, e.g. your boss, a colleague, your neighbour, a friend, etc.

> **EXTRA ACTIVITY**
> Ask students to think of something unusual, but not too unusual, that they have done in their time off. (It can be real or invented.) In pairs or small groups, they should, in turn, tell each other about their activity, using some of the phrases from **2**, but without saying specifically what the activity was. They should start speaking very generally about the activity, and only gradually start including detail, so that the others can guess what the activity is, e.g. :
>
> *After a busy week at work, I finally managed to get away. I'd always wanted to do something different, and challenge myself, so this seemed an ideal opportunity! I've never done that distance before, and I knew the water would be cold too, so I knew it would be difficult. However, it turned out to be a wonderful experience, and we did manage to swim the whole distance. We also made many new friends, too! I don't think I'd do it again, but after the swim we enjoyed a very long drink overlooking the lake!*
> activity = a 'marathon' swim, e.g. across a lake, or a fixed distance (e.g. 5 km).

Language at work

> **DICTIONARY SKILLS**
> Throughout this section, students will find it useful to make use of good dictionaries. Make them aware that if they look up a verb like *want* or *enjoy*, it will tell them if the verb that follows is in the *-ing* or the infinitive form. It will also show common verb patterns following words like *easy* and *worth*.

Exercise 1

Students first read the two instructions, and then answer the question and discuss the change in meaning with reference to the pairs of questions.

> **Answers**
> In sentences 3a and 3b there is little or no change in the meaning. The differences in the rest are explained in **2**.

Exercise 2

Students read the *Language point* and complete the table by referring to the pairs of sentences in **1**.

> **Answers**
>
> | remember (and forget) | 1 *a* | 1 b |
> |---|---|---|
> | go on | 2 a | 2 b |
> | stop | 4 a | 4 b |
> | regret | 5 a | 5 b |

Students will find more information on these and other similar verbs in the *Grammar reference*.

| Grammar reference

| If students need more information, go to *Grammar reference* on page 135 of the *Student's Book*.

Exercise 3

Students underline the correct from of the verb in italics in each sentence.

> **Answers**
> 1 to send   5 not taking
> 2 visiting   6 to bring
> 3 to run   7 to see
> 4 doing

EXTENSION Ask students to find three sentences in **3** which they could use to talk about themselves, but to replace just one or two words, e.g. *Sorry, I didn't remember to send you the newspaper article. I'm late because I stopped to buy a coffee on the way.*

Students work in pairs to tell each other their sentences; encourage listeners to comment, e.g. *It doesn't matter. I found it online. / Oh, I had coffee when I arrived.*

Exercise 4

Students complete the questions 1–4 with the correct form of the verb in brackets and check their answers with a partner.

> **Answers**
> **1** working **2** dealing with **3** to do **4** making

Further practice

If students need more practice, go to *Practice file 15* on page 135 of the *Student's Book*.

Exercise 5

Students work in pairs to consider the questions in **4** as part of a job interview. You could discuss the first question together, e.g. the interviewer wants to know whether the time when you were not working was spent usefully, or not wasted, or perhaps happened because of something personal or otherwise important. A successful candidate would be honest here, and, if they took time off to travel, it would be a good idea to say what they learnt, what experiences they had, how they benefited, etc.

EXTENSION You could ask stronger students or early finishers to think of one more good interview question they could ask, and why.

When they have finished, ask students to report some of their ideas to the group, and encourage others to comment or ask questions.

Then give feedback on any problems with the target verbs. You could put these on the board and ask students, as a class, to correct them.

Photocopiable worksheet

Download and photocopy *Unit 15 Language at work* worksheet from the teacher resources in the *Online practice*.

Talking point

Discussion

Exercise 1

Students read the question and then find the answers in the text.

> **Possible answers**
> Remote Year arrange accommodation and workspace; they also give advice on how to approach the issue at work; you would still get paid (because you are still working); you have the opportunity to travel, etc.

Exercise 2

Students can discuss their ideas with a partner. Elicit some ideas to share with the class and ask students to give reasons for their choices.

Exercise 3

Ask students first to discuss this with a partner, and then elicit some of their ideas to the class, e.g. a boss might initially worry about not having any face-to-face meetings (these could be done online); they might think it's more difficult to check work (this would depend on the nature of the work), etc.

PRE-WORK LEARNERS You could ask students to consider what their tutor would say if they asked for a short-term break (e.g. one to three months) during term time. During this time, the student would continue to stay up-to-date with work (e.g. submit assignments, stay in touch on email / social media forums, etc.).

Suggest students also consider what objections their tutor might have, and how they would address these.

Task

Exercise 1

Students work in pairs to think of suitable questions to ask in an interview situation to recruit for Remote Year, e.g.:

Qualities: *We are looking for people who are self-disciplined and can work alone. Can you give us an example of how you have demonstrated this in the past?*

Skills: *To work remotely, you need to have good IT skills. Describe what you currently use online. How would these skills help you in working remotely?*

Make sure both students make a note of the questions. They will need these for **2**.

PRE-WORK LEARNERS Even if students aren't yet working, they should be able to imagine some of the difficulties which would result from an employee working somewhere else for a year.

Exercise 2

Students swap partners and role-play the interviews, taking it in turn to be the interviewer, and asking the questions prepared in **1**.

ONE-TO-ONE Take turns to role-play the interview. You could use the same questions, or just some of them for each interview. When you have finished, you could together discuss how the interviews went – from the perspective of the candidate, as well as the interviewer: would the candidate be suitable for the Remote Year programme? Why/Why not?

Exercise 3

Students go back to their partner from **1**. They should report back on their interviews and talk about the 'candidate' they interviewed and how suitable they would be for the Remote Year programme.

Progress test

Download and photocopy *Unit 15 Progress test* and *Speaking test* from the teacher resources in the *Online practice*.

Viewpoint 5

Preview

The topic of this *Viewpoint* is *Career perceptions*. Students begin by discussing how career breaks are viewed within their industry and country, and the reasons people take a career break. Students then watch a video about a woman who set up a successful website to help people wanting to take breaks. They then watch a second video about different perceptions and challenges for careers for women. Finally, the students consider their own perceptions of different aspects of careers – career breaks, how companies view them, women in business, climbing the career ladder and so on. Their task then is to challenge each other and try to get others to change their minds to agree with them.

Exercise 1

Ask students to work in small groups. They should first read the questions, and then discuss them as a group. Give them about five minutes. Encourage them to think about a break early on in someone's career, as well as later in life, and perhaps compare how these might differ.

Then elicit a few ideas to share with the whole class. Where appropriate, encourage students to give reasons for their answers.

EXTENSION Ask students if they have any experience or stories about taking a career break.

Exercise 2

Students read the words and phrases 1–8 and match them with the definitions a–h.

After checking the answers, check students can pronounce the following, with the correct word stress: *sabbatical; unconscious bias*.

Answers
1 h 2 e 3 g 4 c 5 f 6 a 7 d 8 b

EXTENSION If you have a weaker group, ask students to work in pairs and think of an example which helps illustrate the meaning of each, e.g. *soft skills* – good communication with people; *perception* – I thought people who took a career break were lazy, but I think that's a very different and wrong perception!

Exercise 3

▶ 01 Give students time to read the topics a–h. They will watch a video about Rachel Morgan-Trimmer, who set up The Career Break Site. Then play the video for them to put the topics in order.

Answers
a 7 b 1 c 2 d 4 e 3 f 6 g 5 h 8

EXTENSION If you have a stronger group, you could ask at this point if students heard anything particularly interesting in the video, and ask them to share it with the others.

Exercise 4

▶ 01 Ask students to read the questions and then play the video again for them to answer them. They then work with a partner to compare their notes.

Answers
1 because she couldn't find a site when she took a career break
2 They want information on options.
3 advice on what to do with your house, your car, and things to take, where to get help
4 volunteering, paid work, travel, TEFL and learning
5 building a school and helping out at a human rights law firm
6 make friends, have a great experience and great memories, and develop confidence
7 learn soft skills
8 They might feel they have flexibility or they might feel they can't lose someone for a period of time.

Check students' answers with the whole class. You may need to explain *TEFL* – teaching English as a foreign language (which some people do for one or two years, as a means of earning while travelling).

Exercise 5

Give students a few minutes to think up their ideas and reasons, and then elicit some to share with the whole class.

PRE-WORK LEARNERS Students can discuss what they would do if they took a longer break between studying and finding a full-time job. Remind them to give reasons for their ideas.

Exercise 6

Ask students to work in small groups. They are going to watch an interview about women's careers with Kathy Harvey at Saïd Business School, who is responsible for academic partnerships. Before they watch, ask them to think about some of the challenges women might face in their careers.

If students need some prompting to get started, elicit or give the following information: women have children, and this can cause interruptions in their career; some women are only expected to do certain jobs, etc.

Give students about five minutes to list their ideas and then regroup them to share their lists and ideas.

Elicit some of the key ideas.

ONE-TO-ONE Brainstorm one or two ideas together first and then you could each make a list, before comparing them.

Exercise 7

▶ **02** Ask students to read the four questions. Then play the video and ask them to put the questions in the order in which the speaker answers them.

Draw students' attention to the *Glossary*.

Answers
a 3 **b** 2 **c** 4 **d** 1

ALTERNATIVE If you have a stronger group, you could ask students to think about their own answers to the questions before playing the video.

Exercise 8

▶ **02** Students read the bullet points, and then watch the video again and take notes. If necessary, pause the video after each section.

Possible answers
The opportunities for women now compared to 30 years ago: nowadays, 50% of university students are female; men and women are fairly equal at the beginning of their careers
The pay gap as you go up the career pipeline: widens as you go up
Women's own perception of themselves: they are often ambitious at first but lack confidence to move up the career ladder
People with a stake in encouraging women in business: families, governments, policymakers, teachers, all of us
Three key factors: confidence, understanding unconscious bias and education

EXTENSION Ask students to consider the information they noted down in the light of their own experience or working environment, e.g. How have employment opportunities changed within their own families? Have they heard about women being paid less in their industry, or amongst their own friends and family?, etc.

Exercise 9

Students work in pairs. They should read the two quotes, and the questions, and discuss them with their partner. Remind them to include reasons for their answers.

After a few minutes, open up the discussion to the whole class.

Exercise 10

Students work on their own. They should read the seven different perceptions of careers and decide how far they agree with each one.

Exercise 11

Ask students to work in small groups. They should first compare how they graded each perception, and then give and listen to each other's reasons for each one. Where possible, they should try to convince others in the group who have a different opinion!

When they have finished, ask one person from each group to summarize their discussions: this could include, first, saying how similar or different the scorings were, and then explaining whether any of them managed to persuade others in the group.

ONE-TO-ONE Individually, you should both score the perceptions on a scale of 1–5. Then share your scores and, in turn, on those issues where you don't agree, try to convince the other person of your own opinion.

EXTRA ACTIVITY
Ask students to work in pairs. They should choose one other person in the class (or you could allocate these, on slips of paper), and decide on a suitable career break for them. They could invent information (e.g. the company they work for, etc.) or make suggestions based on real information. Suggest they consider job types, how the break will be spent (e.g. doing something else at home, travelling, volunteering), how individuals will benefit, what skills they will learn and take back to their company, how the companies will benefit, etc. Try to encourage students to make their ideas as relevant to the individual as possible.

Pre-work learners could consider a six-month break between finishing studies and working.

Further ideas and video scripts
You can find a list of suggested ideas for how to use video in the class in the teacher resources in the *Online practice*. The video scripts are available to download from the Teaching resources on the Oxford Teachers' Club. www.oup.com/elt/teacher/businessresult

Practice file answer key

Unit 1

Working with words

Exercise 1
2 a 3 f 4 d 5 e 6 c 7 h 8 g

Exercise 2
2 trustworthy
3 ineffective
4 functional
5 successful
6 wary
7 modest
8 simple

Business communication

Exercise 1
1 I'm calling about
2 responding so quickly
3 I wondered if you'd
4 I suggest we meet to
5 would you like to meet
6 Let's say
7 Whatever's best
8 in from France, won't you
9 Can you tell me how
10 Let me know where
11 I'll email you a map
12 See you

Exercise 2
1 My name's James Sims and I work for UB.
2 I was given your details by Jill Sander.
3 I wanted to see if you are still interested in our offer.
4 Is it best by taxi or public transport? / Is it best by public transport or taxi?
5 I'll get my assistant to call you later today to confirm. / I'll get my assistant to call you to confirm later today.

Language at work

Exercise 1
1 buys, sells
2 goes
3 does the last flight to New York leave
4 's taking
5 's having
6 'm seeing
7 get back
8 're developing

Exercise 2

Possible answers
2 What does he look like?
3 Do you prefer tea or coffee?
4 What does it taste like?
5 Who does this / it belong to?
6 Do you own your apartment?

Exercise 3
1 catch 2 'm designing 3 'm staying
4 complete 5 check

Unit 2

Working with words

Exercise 1
1 b 2 b 3 a 4 c 5 a 6 b 7 b
8 c 9 a 10 b

Exercise 2
1 feedback
2 appreciation
3 incentive
4 bonus
5 commission
6 fulfilment

Business communication

Exercise 1
2 e 3 d 4 l 5 j 6 f 7 h 8 c
9 i 10 k 11 g 12 a

Exercise 2
1 I don't think we've met.
2 Nice to meet you.
3 What a coincidence!
4 Apparently
5 Really?
6 Well
7 So
8 Catch you later.

Language at work

Exercise 1
1 if / whether (or not) he will take the job
2 when Amanda sent them the catalogue
3 if / whether (or not) this is the train for Munich
4 where the bus for Place de la Concorde goes from
5 if / whether (or not) you've had anything from the minibar
6 who left this package here
7 what time you will be arriving
8 what day is best for you

Exercise 2
1 Aren't you in charge of training?
2 Haven't you completed that report yet?
3 Shouldn't they be here by now?
4 Can't I have my own team working on this?
5 Didn't you want to say something?

Exercise 3
1 aren't you
2 could you
3 doesn't it
4 did you
5 have you
6 will you
7 have they
8 was it

Unit 3

Working with words

Exercise 1
2 stay on track
3 fallen behind schedule
4 an accurate forecast
5 make the launch date
6 budget constraints
7 miss the deadline
8 go over budget

Exercise 2
1 plan 2 run 3 out 4 budget
5 smoothly 6 mess 7 miss
Hidden word = problem

Business communication

Exercise 1
1 b 2 c 3 c 4 c
5 a 6 c 7 b 8 a

Exercise 2
1 d 2 c 3 g 4 f
5 b 6 h 7 e 8 a

Language at work

Exercise 1
1 's decided
2 've already spoken
3 did you see
4 called
5 did he say
6 hasn't made
7 haven't arrived
8 Have you finalized
9 've fixed
10 spoke
11 Have you arranged
12 've just organized
13 booked
14 've been

Exercise 2
1 c 2 a 3 d 4 e 5 f 6 b

Unit 4

Working with words

Exercise 1
1 innovative
2 concept
3 practical
4 technology
5 benefits
6 proposition

Exercise 2
1 set up
2 bring down
3 come up with
4 taken up
5 carried out
6 brought about
7 pay off
8 got round
9 taking forward

Business communication

Exercise 1
2 a 3 e 4 c 5 j
6 b 7 d 8 h 9 i 10 f

Exercise 2
1 whereas
2 The other major advantage
3 is another great thing about
4 At the moment
5 This means
6 The biggest potential benefit of
7 in the future

Language at work

Exercise 1
1 can / will be able to
2 be able to
3 haven't been able to
4 can
5 can
6 be able to
7 can't / won't be able to
8 can't
9 Has she been able to
10 can

Exercise 2

1	could	5	were you able to
2	were you able to	6	couldn't
3	was able to	7	were able to
4	couldn't	8	Were you able to

Unit 5

Working with words

Exercise 1

1 d 2 f 3 c 4 e 5 g 6 a 7 b

Exercise 2

1	Ethical	6	discrimination
2	responsible	7	prejudice
3	credibility	8	bribery
4	generosity	9	corruption
5	fairness	10	deception

Business communication

Exercise 1

2 j 3 b 4 f 5 a 6 h 7 e 8 g
9 d 10 i

Exercise 2

1 We are going to provide you
2 You'll get the opportunity to sample
3 is well worth a visit
4 It would be a good idea to
5 We'd like to invite you to
6 It's just the kind of thing we need
7 Alternatively, we'd be delighted
to show you

Language at work

Exercise 1

Incorrect answers are:

1	I see	5	We will lose
2	I will take	6	I'm being
3	I will meet	7	I'm going to get
4	they are falling		

Exercise 2

1	'm going to pick up	7	Are you staying
2	will be	8	aren't flying
3	'm seeing	9	are you going to get / are you getting
4	'll take		
5	'll make sure	10	leaves
6	're going / 're going to go back	11	only takes
		12	'll have

Unit 6

Working with words

Exercise 1

1	indecisive	5	determined
2	conventional	6	methodical
3	outgoing	7	creative
4	impulsive	8	thoughtful

Exercise 2

1	perspective	5	relying
2	consider	6	confidence
3	weigh up	7	delay
4	between		

Business communication

Exercise 1

1 They're here in black and white …
2 I think it would be crazy to …
3 If you ask me, we should …
4 Could you give us some detail, please?
5 Hang on, let's hear what Clare has to say.
6 What John says is right.
7 If we look at the facts, we'll see …

Exercise 2

1 Today, I'd like to
2 what's your position
3 As far as I'm concerned
4 I don't think we
5 The fact is
6 what you're getting at is
7 I'm not convinced
8 it'll mean we
9 That's my view
10 In other words
11 Let's draw up some action points
12 I don't want to spend too long

Language at work

Exercise 1

countable	uncountable
table	furniture
hotel room	accommodation
week	time
letter	correspondence
computer program	software
photocopier	equipment
lesson	training
euro	money

Exercise 2

1 is 2 were 3 don't 4 is
5 has 6 aren't 7 was 8 is

Exercise 3

1	more	5	very few
2	a	6	some
3	is very little	7	very little
4	too many	8	a morning paper

Unit 7

Working with words

Exercise 1

1	activities	5	workers
2	process	6	growth
3	home	7	location
4	facility		

Exercise 2

1 leads to job losses
2 improved the quality of life for
3 take cost-cutting measures
4 streamline our operation
5 free up resources
6 created (980) new jobs
7 gain a competitive edge

Business communication

Exercise 1

1	data	3	look at
2	has resulted in	4	move on

5	Due	9	turn our attention to
6	notice on		
7	a result	10	the facts
8	looked at	11	Have a
		12	leave

Exercise 2

1 to 2 of 3 to 4 at 5 in 6 on
7 to 8 of 9 to 10 for

Language at work

Exercise 1

1 All my important files have been lost.
2 my flat had been broken into
3 to be promoted
4 being told
5 Our computer system must have been hacked into.
6 we are not being told
7 I'm being sent
8 the chairs were being put away
9 Microsoft's latest operating system was unveiled
10 the Olympic Village will be closed

Exercise 2

1	accuses	11	have had
2	are paid	12	have been made
3	don't recognize	13	have always produced
4	are often forced		
5	visited	14	have benefited
6	was told	15	will be raised
7	were	16	'll get
8	were given	17	'll keep up
9	made	18	will finally be done
10	was packed		

Unit 8

Working with words

Exercise 1

1 h 2 f 3 a 4 d
5 g 6 c 7 e 8 b

Exercise 2

1	unemployable	6	operational / operations
2	apprenticeship		
3	retirement	7	management
4	unprofitable	8	satisfaction
5	owners		

Business communication

Exercise 1

1 c 2 b 3 d 4 c 5 d 6 b 7 a
8 c 9 d 10 b

Exercise 2

1 The areas we need to discuss are
2 One option would be to
3 Why don't we take on
4 So what have we got so far
5 That sounds like a plan

Language at work

Exercise 1

1	want, will	5	will, give
2	wanted, would	6	would, spoke
3	were, would	7	were, would
4	would, had	8	want, can

Exercise 2
1 first conditional: 1, 5, 8
2 second conditional: 2, 3, 4, 6, 7

Exercise 3
1 in case 2 unless 3 Provided
4 if 5 As long

Exercise 4
Possible answers
1 I would take a year off
2 I knew I could get my job back
3 I'll go for a walk
4 we'll start without him

Unit 9
Working with words
Exercise 1
1 c 2 b 3 a 4 c 5 c 6 b 7 b
8 c 9 a 10 b

Exercise 2
1 totally 6 helpful
2 extremely 7 impossible
3 absolutely 8 very
4 incredibly 9 terrible
5 clever 10 completely

Business communication
Exercise 1
1 What **are you doing** here?
2 I **haven't seen** you for ages.
3 How's **life treating** you?
4 How's **business with you**?
5 … could you **do** me a favour?
6 The thing is, I'**m looking for** someone …
7 That's not something I can **decide** on right now.
8 I'll **certainly** think about it.

Exercise 2
1 j 2 e 3 i 4 c 5 d 6 b 7 h
8 a 9 g 10 f

Language at work
Exercise 1
1 've known 6 've been going
2 's been staying sailing
3 has been using 7 've had
4 've been 8 have you been
negotiating waiting
5 've been reading / 9 've been trying
've read 10 's been raining

Exercise 2
1 i 2 d 3 b 4 f 5 g 6 a 7 c
8 e 9 h 10 j

Unit 10
Working with words
Exercise 1
1 into 2 to 3 on 4 on 5 on
6 on 7 about 8 with 9 with

Exercise 2
1 analyst 6 developers
2 analytical 7 consultation
3 communicative 8 consultants
4 communication 9 economists
5 economize 10 developments

Business communication
Exercise 1
1 How can I help you
2 Could you explain exactly what the problem is
3 Let me get this straight
4 by tomorrow
5 Could you give me
6 Once I've looked into it I'll call you back
7 You mean
8 in time for the

Exercise 2
1 What can I do **for you**?
2 If I understand you **correctly** …
3 I'll look **into** it straightaway.
4 We need the goods in time **for** …
5 … I'll get **back to you**.
6 … by Friday **at** the latest.

Language at work
Exercise 1
2 Can you look over this report for me?
3 Please drop the package off before lunchtime. / Please drop off the package before lunchtime.
4 She called me over for a quick chat.
5 I'm just showing these people round the factory.
6 Have you given up smoking yet? / Have you given smoking up yet?
7 He's out of the office, but I can put you through to his voicemail.
8 I don't think we managed to get our main message across. / I don't think we managed to get across our main message.
9 They've looked through the spreadsheet in detail.
10 I wouldn't count on them agreeing to that price.

Exercise 2
1 read back 6 set up
2 came across as 7 weigh up
3 put it off 8 carry out
4 Hang up 9 count on
5 laid off 300 people

Unit 11
Working with words
Exercise 1
1 support 5 achieve
2 react 6 implement
3 affect 7 maintain
4 revert 8 prevent

Exercise 2
2 hostile 6 optimistic
3 critical 7 concerned
4 ambivalent 8 enthusiastic
5 receptive

Business communication
Exercise 1
1 as you all know
2 Starting from February next year
3 We'd like to assure you
4 we're calling on you to
5 we are fairly certain everyone
6 You may be wondering
7 I'd like to pass this point over to
8 let's digress for a moment and

Exercise 2
1 Starting from next month we'll be learning
2 We're well aware of your concerns regarding
3 Over the next few weeks we'll be nominating
4 We're also proposing to introduce
5 Veronika will now deal with
6 Later this month we'll be recruiting

Language at work
Exercise 1
1 'll be talking 7 won't have
2 'll have finished agreed
3 'll be analysing 8 'll be visiting
4 'll have published 9 'll be attending
5 'll also be 10 won't have got
holding back
6 will be giving

Exercise 2
2 To be honest, I probably won't get the job.
3 They are quite likely to cancel the whole order.
4 There are certain to be some changes in the final design.
5 They are unlikely to accept these terms.
6 I think I might be offered a promotion.
7 We may face some opposition to these changes.
8 If this goes ahead, there will definitely be some job losses.

Unit 12
Working with words
Exercise 1
1 age 5 behaviour
2 driven 6 history
3 analytics 7 demographics
4 gather

Exercise 2
1 c 2 f 3 d 4 a 5 e 6 g
7 b 8 h

Business communication
Exercise 1
1 speaking 5 interpret
2 According 6 low-down
3 figures 7 general
4 bottom

Exercise 2

1 Can we look at the figures
2 In general
3 According to
4 What's that in terms of
5 Stani assured us that
6 Apparently, figures from
7 show
8 overall, things are looking

Language at work

Exercise 1

1 (that) the plan would not work
2 (that) (s)he doesn't believe in working at weekends
3 if I could send the letter
4 how long I had been waiting
5 (that) they had had a great time on holiday
6 what she thought about the proposal
7 (that) a lot of people are unhappy about the changes
8 (that) he hadn't shown anyone the plans yet
9 if she had ever been skiing
10 (that) he'll be back on Friday

Exercise 2

1 (that) the project was progressing well
2 (that) they would probably finish stage one by the end of that week
3 (that) the three construction firms were going to begin work on the stadium the following week
4 (that) they had originally budgeted for two construction firms
5 (that) the timing of the project had meant that they had needed to contract another (contractor)
6 (that) they could finish (the project) on time

Unit 13

Working with words

Exercise 1

1 individualistic   6 cautious
2 liberal   7 formal
3 egalitarian   8 strict
4 hierarchical   9 open
5 accepting   10 collectivist

Exercise 2

1 to 2 of 3 about 4 with
5 of 6 to 7 to 8 of

Business communication

Exercise 1

1 in the end
2 It came about because of
3 That was the first problem
4 So what did you do
5 It seems that
6 What happened next
7 that was when I felt really uncomfortable
8 As time went by

Exercise 2

1 At first   5 Luckily
2 What's more   6 It really surprised
3 It wasn't until   me, but it
4 Despite   worked.

Language at work

Exercise 1

1 didn't recognize, 'd changed
2 was waiting, called
3 was, was raining
4 met, was working
5 got, 'd left
6 arrived, had been broken
7 jumped, ran, smashed
8 noticed, was reading

Exercise 2

1 was doing   12 turned
2 went   13 ran
3 arrived   14 looked
4 decided   15 was racing
5 was walking   16 was chasing
6 saw   17 reached
7 stopped   18 dived
8 'd never come   19 looked
9 didn't know   20 was
10 jumped   21 had disappeared
11 came   22 were laughing

Unit 14

Working with words

Exercise 1

1 monitor   5 express
2 conduct   6 constructive
3 address   7 raise / address
4 objective

Exercise 2

1 Performance   5 form
2 appraisals   6 value
3 tool   7 peer
4 criteria

Exercise 3

1 out 2 through 3 on
4 over / across 5 on 6 with

Business communication

Exercise 1

1 successes 2 failures 3 have been
4 happy 5 improve 6 best way 7 ought

Exercise 2

1 **Feedback** from ...
2 How **should I do this**
3 Can we **identify** that as
4 we could **do** with some support
5 you **demonstrated** good
6 I **wouldn't** have organized
7 While we're talking **about** money

Language at work

Exercise 1

1 'd bought, would have made
2 would have missed, 'd driven
3 'd studied, wouldn't need

4 had gone on, would have shut down
5 hadn't brought, wouldn't be talking
6 'd packed, would have happened
7 'd left, would be
8 'd been, would have done

Exercise 2

1 You could have been dismissed.
2 You could have seen Anne.
3 You shouldn't have spoken
4 You could / might / should have let me know
5 You should have sent
6 We could have lost
7 You could / might / should have called

Unit 15

Working with words

Exercise 1

1 perspective   5 put off
2 appreciate   6 charity
3 hesitate   7 revitalized
4 tip

Exercise 2

1 enthusiasm   5 broaden
2 Soft   6 head off
3 development   7 policy
4 retention
Hidden word = holiday

Business communication

Exercise 1

1 a 2 c 3 c 4 b 5 d 6 b
7 d 8 b

Exercise 2

1 It's been a long-term goal of mine to finish my university course.
2 The plus points are skills development and more leadership experience.
3 My motivation for this comes from my volunteer work with the Red Cross.
4 I'll never be satisfied unless I do it.
5 That's hardly fair – I've never refused to do overtime.

Language at work

Exercise 1

1 to tell   10 to give
2 to do   11 to keep
3 to think   12 taking
4 finding   13 working
5 to be sent   14 to check
6 to oversee   15 collaborating
7 to be   16 to discuss
8 to explore   17 hearing
9 letting

Exercise 2

1 a 2 f 3 c 4 h 5 d 6 e
7 g 8 b